Life Is Spiritual Practice

LIFE
IS
SPIRITUAL
PRACTICE

Achieving Happiness
with the 10 Perfections

Jean Smith

WISDOM PUBLICATIONS • BOSTON

Wisdom Publications
199 Elm Street
Somerville, MA 02144 USA
www.wisdompubs.org

Library of Congress Cataloging-in-Publication Data
Smith, Jean, 1938– author.
  Life is spiritual practice : achieving happiness through the ten perfections / Jean Smith.
    pages cm
  Includes bibliographical references and index.
  ISBN 1-61429-157-8 (pbk. : alk. paper) — ISBN 978-1-61429-173-2 (ebook)
  1. Paramitas (Buddhism) 2. Spiritual life—Buddhism. I. Title.
  BQ4336.S63 2015
  294.3'444—dc23

                    2014020579

ISBN 978-1-61429-157-2   ebook ISBN 978-1-61429-173-2

19 18 17 16 15
5 4 3 2 1

Cover design by Laura Shaw. Interior design by Gopa&Ted2, Inc. Set in Hoefler 10.3/15.2.

Wisdom Publications' books are printed on acid-free paper and meet the guidelines for permanence and durability of the Production Guidelines for Book Longevity of the Council on Library Resources.

This book was produced with environmental mindfulness. We have elected to print this title on 30% PCW recycled paper. As a result, we have saved the following resources: 10 trees, 5 million BTUs of energy, 886 lbs. of greenhouse gases, 4,808 gallons of water, and 322 lbs. of solid waste. For more information, please visit our website, www.wisdompubs.org.

Printed in the United States of America.

Please visit www.fscus.org.

Contents

Introduction:
So You Want to Be Happy

MAHATMA GANDHI believed that happiness is natural when what you think, what you say, and what you do are in harmony. Such astute assertions often lead us to counter with responses like "Yes, but does *everything* have to be an experience for learning harmony?" or "Oh no, not *another* unasked-for growth opportunity!" or "I don't want any more spiritual challenges." When such thoughts come up, they're usually unenthusiastic reactions to situations in our everyday lives—times when we're not in harmony. But, in fact, those situations *can* be learning experiences and growth opportunities—even cornerstones of our spiritual life and happiness: Every aspect of our lives, even the most mundane, can be part of our spiritual practice.

Let me share a very old story with you. Thousands of years ago two young men who had grown up together decided to go their separate ways in adulthood. Unknown to the younger one, the older sewed a precious jewel into the lining of the younger's coat. Years later they met again. The older man had prospered, but the younger had fallen on hard times, and his clothing was in tatters. The older man shocked him by showing him the hidden jewel and telling him that this wealth had always been available to him, had he but known of it.

Each one of us carries such precious stones. They are sacred jewels of purity in our hearts, known as the *paramis*, or perfections. If we want everyday life to be spiritually rewarding to ourselves and others, we need only realize that they are there and that we can bring them to light.

This possibility of living a seamless life—one that embraces the jewels in all aspects of our lives, rather than sewing them into separate pockets for work, relationships, play, faith, and such—is what peaked my interest in spirituality, one day in 1984 when I encountered a way of life I'd spent years searching for.

I was in the Himalayas that day; I'd walked into a small Nepali village of about seven houses. I paused, as I usually did, near the well, to get a sense of this community and its people. After about twenty minutes I wandered on until I saw a woman sitting on her mud stoop, weaving on a vertical loom. I had never seen anyone use a vertical loom but the Athabascan people of North America, whom the weaver very much resembled physically. I squatted down near her, my head filled with intellectual analyses about migration between Asia and North America and Ice Ages.

Then the weaver looked up at me and smiled. I smiled back, brought my hands together, and said, "*Namaste*"—"the spirit in me salutes the spirit in you." She bowed with her hands together and responded, "*Namaste*." I looked at her weaving and said, "*Ramro*"—"beautiful." She smiled again, then turned her attention back to her loom. I stayed there, watching her. As the minutes passed, I observed that she was totally absorbed by what she was doing. Her quiet purposefulness inspired a sense of serenity in me—I realized that she had something I did not fully understand but knew I wanted. She was my first teacher of Buddhism: she showed me that even the most ordinary daily activity is an opportunity for spiritual practice. Such absorption is possible no matter what the setting—one doesn't have to be a Himalayan villager to see life in front of you as a source of practice. But, you may ask, "Why would we *want* to make life our spiritual practice anyway?" To cite the Dalai Lama's answer: because all beings want to be happy—*all* beings, whether a child staring through the window of a toy store wanting to get inside or a housefly banging against a window trying to get outside. When we look back throughout history, we find that the people who most successfully have found the true nature of happiness and shared it with others—whether Jesus of Nazareth, Nelson Mandela of South Africa, or Aung San Suu Kyi of Burma—have been seen as "good people." Historical period, ethnic group, gender, culture, and faith have not determined who these people are. Each has embodied characteristics of heart and mind that others have recognized and emulated. Meditation teacher Steve Armstrong described these heart-mind characteristics in modern terminology as "default settings for first responders to suffering." And you have these settings built in too.

All faiths and religions have shining exemplars of the kind of people we would like to be. In the framework for this book, I have chosen the teachings of the Buddha, for three primary reasons: First, the systematic study of the ten heart-mind qualities (the perfections) that led Siddartha Gautama to be recognized as the Buddha have been scrutinized for almost 2,600 years and are well documented. Second, the Buddha emphasized that these qualities of the heart are ones that *we already have and can learn to develop further*. Third, these ten qualities are not inherently Buddhist characteristics—they are human ideals, natural and sacred in all of us.

If any of the Buddhist material in this book does not resonate with you, that's just fine. Plumb your own spiritual tradition for similar teachings. The Buddha himself stressed that we should not take what he says as absolute truth but rather as propositions that we ourselves should test and "prove" to ourselves. We don't have to seek out esoteric teachings or philosophies to make our daily lives into our spiritual practice; all we have to do is embrace four goals:

1. Establish the heartfelt intention to want to lead a "good" life.
2. Identify the heart-mind qualities we want to actualize.
3. Cultivate mindfulness to recognize the presence or absence of those qualities.
4. Resolve to make those qualities central to our lives.

A warning: This path is not an instant bliss trip. The contentment and fulfillment we can achieve don't come to us in a spiritual hot flash but rather must be cultivated slowly over time. This means that the first step on the path is faith: believing that you *can* be happy but not at others' expense. Part I, "Foundations for Happiness," explores the practices that inspire and confirm this faith, the ways we can learn to deal with life on life's terms—and to do so with equanimity. Key among these foundations is mindful awareness of the heart-mind characteristics that lead to our spiritual liberation, ideals introduced in chapter 5.

The second step is willingness to cultivate these spiritual practices in our everyday life. Throughout the book, the strategies for happiness are applied to specific areas of life, such as relationships, work, and illness. Each chapter in part II delineates a particular ideal and begins with a resolve that when nurtured perfects that ideal, as well as a shortened version, a mantra, that may be used in meditation practice.

The word *practice* is important here. Think about some kinds of practice: Vocalists don't spend hours singing scales so that they can go out on stage and sing scales. Tennis players don't spend hours hitting a ball against a wall so that they can enter a tournament where they hit balls against a wall. Those seeking physical fitness don't spend hours lifting weights so that they can go out onto the street and lift weights for the entertainment of passersby. Similarly, we don't practice mindful awareness so that we can take a meditation cushion out in public so people can admire our sitting technique. The "performance" of our practice is making our lives into the basis of spiritual integrity, an endeavor that can lead us to freedom and happiness and a way of living that does not harm others or our world.

We can achieve these blessings by embracing and developing the perfections of the Buddha. Join me in bringing them to light in your life; join me in taking the steps to make these ten resolves central to our lives:

1. Generosity: May my heart be open to give and to receive
with joy and ease.

2. Ethical Integrity: May ethical integrity in thoughts, words,
and actions be my gift to myself and the beings around me.

3. Renunciation: May I let go of anything that harms me
or other beings.

4. Wisdom: May I make insightful choices that lead to compassion and liberation for all.

5. Wise Effort: May I awaken and sustain spiritual ideals in my life.

6. Patience: May I be patient and forgiving when negative emotions and events arise.

7. Truthfulness: May I be truthful with myself and others.

8. Resolve: May I resolve that my spiritual practice is for the benefit of all beings.

9. Loving-Kindness: May loving-kindness define my relationships with others.

10. Equanimity: Balanced in body, heart, and mind, may I be nonreactive to the unexpected changes of life.

Jean Smith
Taos, New Mexico

Part I
Foundations for Happiness

1.
Suffering as the Beginning of Happiness

THE BUDDHA FREQUENTLY SAID, "I teach one thing and one thing only: suffering and the end of suffering." If his sentence had ended after the first time the word *suffering* was used, his teachings probably would have lasted about 26 minutes instead of 2,600 years. But from his first teaching, he said that suffering has a cause and *can be ended*. When we are honest with ourselves, we know deep in our hearts that life is more often uncomfortable than not and that we spend a lot of time, money, and energy trying to get rid of discomfort. But none of our solutions seems to last very long or to be totally satisfying.

As a basis for all that follows, let's begin with an overview of some key points regarding suffering and happiness, drawn from the Buddha's first teaching, on the Four Noble Truths. A first challenge is in using the word *suffering*. Among the more popular translations of the Pali word *dukkha*, which the Buddha used for suffering, are "dis-ease," "stress," and "anguish." The causes of this dis-ease include "birth, aging, illness, death, having to be with what one does not like, not getting what one wants, craving what one doesn't have or clinging to what one has." All suffering is possible only through contact with our six senses (the mind is included as a sense). The end of suffering is nonattachment or nonclinging, which requires wisdom, moral integrity, and mental discipline. Interestingly, the origin of the word *dukkha* was the hole through which a chariot's axle passed, so not all dukkha was of the life-and-death variety—if you've ever had a grocery cart with a clunky wheel, you've known dukkha.

These initial teachings are straightforward and from the Buddha's keystone teaching, the Four Noble Truths: dis-ease is part of life, its cause is clinging, its end is to relinquish clinging, and there is a path to the end of clinging. But to complicate matters, the Buddha described all conditioned existence (which means everything in life, because all life depends upon causes and conditions) as comprising three characteristics: suffering, impermanence, and not-self (the absence of a permanent, autonomous, separate self). We'll look closely at each of these characteristics in more detail later, but first let's isolate just one aspect: craving what we have come into contact with through our senses. When we realize that (1) dis-ease is caused by attachment through our senses and that (2) our senses too—like all conditioned things—are impermanent, we get an inkling of why even the things that at least momentarily make us most happy are in themselves the source of future dis-ease. In other words, when we who are impermanent cling to that which is also impermanent, eventually we will experience dis-ease, because those cherished objects of our attachment (people, situations, emotions, even ideas) will change or end. For example, if we see a chocolate ice cream bar, we may begin to experience a craving for chocolate, then eat the whole bar, then feel sadness when we have eaten it and it is gone. Understanding the nature and effects of impermanence is critical to our being willing to take the steps necessary to nurture our spiritual lives.

Although we may become attached to almost anything that we contact through the senses, four areas of attachment often cause the greatest suffering:

1. **Clinging to sense pleasures**. Sometimes our clinging to sights, sounds, smells, tastes, and tactile sensations becomes so powerful that it is a passion, an addiction. The first twelve-step program, Alcoholics Anonymous, was founded to deal with the seemingly hopeless addiction to alcohol. Now there are twelve-step programs for a range of sense addictions from narcotics to sex to food. Many of us have had the experience of gaining such pleasure from overindulging in our favorite food or drink that we have made ourselves sick, or at least

unhealthy. Addiction is a complex psychological and physical phenomenon; I am not suggesting that addiction is as simple as thinking about wine or chocolate ice cream as being delicious. Because in Buddhism the brain is considered a sense organ, the combination of a physical addiction and a mental obsession can make the dynamics of a strong craving hard to resist.

2. **Clinging to ideas and opinions about the world and the "narratives" of our lives.** Discomfort around our opinions about the world seems to ratchet up considerably during election years. Observe what happens to your body and mind, for example, when you watch a presidential debate on TV. And observe yourself and those around you when your candidate loses, even if only for the school board.

3. **Clinging to precepts, rites, and practices.** The degree to which we can become attached to particular ways of doing things—"the right, the *only* way"—historically has shown up, sometimes violently, when a religious practice has been violated or even modified. There was anger, chaos, and rebellion, for example, when the Catholic Church started saying Mass in the vernacular of a country rather than in Latin. Depicting the Prophet Muhammad in a graphic representation has evoked enraged protests from Muslims around the world. Adherents of one school of Buddhism may scoff because another school meditates too much, or not enough. Even in everyday life, clinging to "our way" can cause us some degree of discomfort over such commonplace acts as a guest helping with after-dinner cleanup who does not wash the glasses first, a child who leaves a favorite book on the bed rather than a shelf, not having turkey for Thanksgiving dinner, forgetting to celebrate a spouse's birthday.

4. **Clinging to the dogma of a separate, permanent self.** Philosophers, without experiencing a great deal of suffering, may speculate intellectually about the existence of a self and its defining characteristics. ("I think, therefore I am"; if I don't think, am I not?) But for the rest of us, anytime a situation arouses an aversive reaction—fear, anger, blame, jealousy, feelings of inadequacy—we suffer. Each aversive emotion—and some seemingly positive ones (such as joy at our success)—separate

us from the other beings in our world. The result is dis-ease based on delusion, which we shall look at more closely in chapter 4.

To summarize: within whatever makes us happy is the seed of suffering, if we become attached, because both the object of our happiness and ourselves are impermanent. With deeper understanding comes the great comfort that the thing itself is not what makes us unhappy; how we relate to it—attachment or its converse, aversion—causes the discomfort. The very good news (and sometimes seemingly impossible task) is that dis-ease will end, and we will achieve lasting liberation from suffering, if only we change our attitude toward everything in the world, including ourselves.

Lest this seem an impossible quest, let me share a metaphor from the Thai meditation teacher Ajaan Suwat. When he wanted to explain to a student how he or she could ease stress from the situations in life, Ajaan Suwat would ask if a mountain is heavy. When the student replied that certainly a mountain is heavy, Ajaan would say that even if it is, it is only heavy if we try to lift it and carry it around. So our equanimity lies in acknowledging the existence of problems, solving them when we can, but learning how not to let them burden our heart if we can't.

Just as initial happiness can lead to suffering, so too can happiness spring from suffering when we change the way we relate to suffering, when we don't try to lift and cling to our problems. And that is how we transform our lives.

The introduction stressed that the first steps in making our whole lives our spiritual path are having faith in the possibility of transformation and willingness to spend the necessary time in mindfulness practice. This chapter adds that we must acknowledge and seek understanding of Buddha's three basic truths: the truth of suffering (including its origin, cessation, and path to cessation), impermanence, and not-self. In chapter 9, we will discuss that we also must make a commitment to live a life of nonharming, the ethical basis that underlies all spirituality.

Here are some basic realizations that make it possible to start on this path:

1. First, we must realize that it's not the events and conditions in our life that make us happy or unhappy but rather how we relate to them. An old bumper sticker said: "Shit Happens." Wrong: "Life Happens," to all of us. When we acknowledge that how we relate to what happens to us can cause suffering or not, we become willing to cultivate traits like equanimity, to see things clearly, and to let go of delusions such as "You'd be miserable too, if you had to endure this." Which leads to a second important realization:

2. The events and conditions of life are not personal. We have not been singled out to grow old, get sick, die, lose a loved one, or any of the other things that bring us suffering. In one popular metaphor, rain falls equally on all of us. Again, the trick is how we relate to it. Do we melt, or do we open an umbrella? Which leads to a third point:

3. We have a choice as to what action we take or don't. In Bhikkhu Bodhi's translation of Majjhima Nikaya 135, the Buddha stressed, "Beings are owners of their actions, heirs of their actions, they originate from their actions, are bound to their actions, have their actions as their refuge." What he was talking about here is karma, our *intentional* acts, explored in detail in chapter 3. All our karmic actions will have consequences when the conditions for their fruition are right. Nothing is ever lost. We cannot change our past karma. But if we are mindful in the present moment—which is the only time we have choices—we can affect our future karma. A piercing expression of this truth is a phrase commonly used in an equanimity meditation: "You are the owner of your karma, the heir of your karma. Your happiness depends upon *your* actions, not upon my good wishes for you." In other words, if you open the umbrella, you won't get wet. But many of us cling to our umbrella without opening it, which leads to a fourth point:

4. Like an old country song says, "I'm looking for love in all the wrong places." We tend to single out something—a person, a job, a vacation, the right deodorant—that will make us happy. And we cling to it as if it exists as a permanent, unchangeable cure-all. But as we've stressed, there's suffering when we who are impermanent become attached to that which is also impermanent. Which leads to a fifth point:

5. There's no such thing as a permanent self. Each of us is empty of a separate, autonomous, unchanging self—the statement "I went to Finland fifteen years ago" is meaningless: there's not a cell in the body or a thought or an emotion that was present both then and now. And everything else is also impermanent—something particle physicists seem to grasp. When we don't understand this truth we fulfill meditation teacher Joseph Goldstein's observation that if there's anyone home to suffer, they will. *This* leads to a sixth truth:

6. We're all in this together. If we're not separate, we're together. One of my favorite expressions of this is the story of the mythical Indra's Net, which surrounds the universe and has a multifaceted jewel at every crossing, so that every jewel reflects every other jewel and is reflected in every other jewel. This is a beautiful image that mirrors the intricacy of interrelationships among us. There's another, more earthy old teaching story that describes interrelationships another way: There was a garden of melons behind a monk's hut—but not ordinary melons. They had faces like jack-o-lanterns, and they had little arms and hands growing out of each side. One day, the melons started "selfing"—each one insisted that it was different, better, the finest melon of all. Tempers escalated as each melon tried to convince the others that it was supreme. Things got so vehement that the melons were beginning to close their fists and threaten each other. About that time, the monk came out and observed what was happening. The melons looked at each other and then at the monk, not quite sure what to do next. The monk said quietly, "I want each of you to open your fists and place your hands right on top of your heads." When the melons did this, they discovered the vines that joined them all to each other.

Thus, to make our whole lives our spiritual practice, we need faith that this is possible, and we need willingness to work with the three basic life truths: suffering, impermanence, and not-self. These truths teach us that how we relate to the circumstances of our lives determines our level of suffering, that the challenges in life are not personal to us, that by being mindful in the present moment we can determine our future karma, and that because there is no separate permanent self, we are all interrelated.

I've outlined here these teachings as if they were linear instead of a holographic spiral. To see how the "foundations" outlined in this chapter might play out in some areas of our lives, let's look at the first area the Buddha defined as dukkha—aging—then look at some ways you can reflect on your own aging.

Aging: Impermanent, Impersonal

Aging, with its concomitant physical and mental changes, happens to all of us. Whether aging brings suffering or happiness depends upon how we relate to it. When we're children, we're delighted to add another mark to the doorway to show how much we've grown; we come home excited because we've memorized a multiplication table. Fast forward some decades to the time we go in for an annual physical exam, are measured, and are told that we're an inch shorter than we used to be—or when we stumble trying to remember a word or name, having a "senior moment." Somehow we're surprised, as if we thought these changes happened to others but could never happen to us.

Just as we may experience glee when we are "old enough to…" at other times, we react with anger or guilt or puzzlement when we realize that we are "too old to…" A friend once came over for coffee, raging and at the same time shame-ridden. She summed up what was happening by saying, "I realize when I walk down the street that I'm so old that men don't notice me any more." This *is* an opportunity for spiritual growth when we can see how attached we are to looking a particular way and getting the approval—or at least the attention—of others.

The first time I got a real sense of aging, I was at a health club waiting for an exercise class to begin. I was standing with my teacher outside a classroom where a dance aerobics class was going on; the people inside were throwing themselves about in a frenzy. My teacher said, "It looks like they're really having fun." I said, "Yeah, but I think I'd be self-conscious doing that." She said, "Ummm, the first time my mom came to one of my classes, she felt that way too." I suddenly realized that she had put me into the same category as her mother—and that I belonged there. I felt mortified. When had this happened? About the same time I had to put on glasses not just to read the phone book but also to eat a meal.

When we're young, we may be happy to have physically matured enough to compete in certain sports or to ride roller coasters. But as we get beyond a certain age, we begin to be more limited in what we can do physically. When I was no longer able to hike up mountains—one of my favorite pastimes—I had the choice to just sit there in the valley or to find an alternative. I bought a horse who could go up into the mountains and a ladder so that I could get on her. I opened the umbrella.

I remember the first time I went to an aquatic aerobics class with all the other "ancients." It seemed to be the only kind of exercise I could still do. My first thought was "Has it come to this?" and when I realized realistically that it *had* come to that, I settled in and enjoyed the classes. At one point the instructor put on a tape of music from the 1960s. You should have seen this pool full of old gals, gray heads thrown back, singing every word, making vortexes in the water as we did a bit of the dirty boogie from our younger days. One woman commented that it was a good thing we couldn't fall down in the water. That day, I experienced impermanence through physical changes, saw these changes in everyone around me and acknowledged that they were not personal, detached from "the way I used to be," and enjoyed myself thoroughly.

One goal of spiritual practice is to see the world and ourselves in it clearly. When we have expectations that for the rest of our lives we'll be able to do everything we could at some magic age—say, thirty-five—we are simply being delusional. We have opportunities throughout our lives to observe impermanence as we age. We see the choices we have about our lifestyles as we age. We see these things in others. We can look back over our lives and be grateful for all the wonderful moments we've had, and we can come into the present moment with gratitude for the accomplishments, wisdom, and compassion we could only have achieved with life experience during the passing of time.

Practice and Reflection: Aging

Take a few minutes now to explore your relationship to aging.

- Can you think of a time when you became sharply aware of your own aging? How old were you? Did it make you happy or unhappy? What universal principles—suffering, impermanence, "selfing"—can you learn from that particular experience?

- Outside of your family, are the people you choose to spend time with about your age or older or younger? Why do you make this choice?

- How has your relationship to your career changed as you've aged?

- What are your current interests and pastimes? Have they changed as you've aged? Why or why not?

- What is the most challenging aspect of aging for you today? How can you change your relationship to it so that it will be less stressful?

- Close your eyes and reflect for ten minutes on how aging can be an opportunity for practice in your life.

2.
Impermanence and the Self: The Beginning of Suffering

WE CAN STUDY DISCOURSES and sermons, we can read countless books, we can hear hundreds or perhaps even thousands of talks. Although these secondary sources give us many clues about the nature of our world, only direct experience can give us true insight into two of the most essential aspects of our reality: impermanence and the nonexistence of a permanent, autonomous self. Familiarity with these insights is necessary for the "real life" practices in part II. But how do we learn about these challenging realities? By directly experiencing them.

Most of us have heard and conceded the adage that we can't step in the same river twice, but until we wade into a stream and feel the current swirling around our calves as it urges leaves and twigs past us, we do not really get, at a kinetic level, what this saying means. And we are just like that stream. Each of us is made up of and surrounded by elements that are constantly changing. As Zen teacher Jisho Warner has said, "Impermanence is a great river of phenomena, of beings, things, and events, coming to be and passing away in dependence on each other. This natural order of things includes us, and its laws are our laws. Each of us is an endless moving stream within an endless moving stream."

For twenty years I had a home on the Ausable River, in the Adirondack Mountains of Upstate New York, and that river was a wily teacher. I came to understand that being a moving stream in a moving stream does not mean that our lives flow through without changing or being changed. Over the years I watched the river carve the shoreline, carrying sand downstream as it widened meanders, making sandbars in the already broad and shallow areas. I saw the river's color changed by the shore, where iron-rich clays narrowed the channel. The water rose and fell with rains in the mountains, carried whole trees downstream in the fury of a flood, buckled bridges with crusted ice. But even in the most bitter frozen winterscape, always through the ice I could see the river's flow.

The river of beings' existence, according to the Buddha, comprises five flowing "collectives" or "aggregates" (*skandhas* in Sanskrit): material form, feeling, perception, mental formations (thoughts and emotions), and consciousness, and he uses dramatic similes to illustrate their insubstantial nature. He compares material form to a lump of foam, feeling to a bubble, perception to a mirage, mental formations to the trunk of a banana tree (which is pithless, without heartwood), and consciousness to an illusion, and asks: "What essence could there be in a lump of foam, in a bubble, in a mirage, in a banana trunk, in an illusion?" Another metaphor used by a friend is standing at the edge of a river and studying the small whirlpools that form then fade away. There is no difference between the river and the whirlpools except the whirlpools' temporary coherence: existing, changing, not existing.

When we look at a mountain or at our own reflection in the mirror, the ephemeral nature of all beings and of the very world we live in may be difficult to grasp. Changes are so slow and so subtle, or sometimes so fast and so subtle, that objects and beings appear permanent, solid. But all conditioned things—that is, all things that depend upon causes and conditions for existence, which amounts to *all* things and beings— are ever-changing. As more and more powerful microscopes have been invented, the less scientists think there is some true, indivisible "building block" of matter: even the smallest identifiable particles are in flux.

I find it remarkable that long before there were microscopes, the Buddha understood this truth. In fact, impermanence is not just one of the three root characteristics of reality described by the Buddha; it is the basis of the other two (suffering and not-self): the self, which seems so real and permanent to us, is nothing more than five ever-changing collectives. Phrased another way, as we've noted, when we who are impermanent cling to that which is also impermanent, the only possible result is suffering. We must realize that our senses and our brains, our only sources of knowledge about the world, are impermanent material-form collectives, and we must recall the Buddha's observation that "with our minds we make the world."

I am a verb, not a noun. I am a process, not a thing. Yet so often we feel like an "I"; we feel as if we and others exist as separate entities. We recognize our faces in the mirror and our friends when we see them. To respond to this, the Buddha asked if an exact painting of a person is that person, or if the image in a mirror is the person reflected. In our ability to recognize objects and beings, relatively speaking we do exist, but not as a permanent phenomenon separate from and independent of all others. These "feelings of self" are mental formations and reliance on the memory characteristic of consciousness, both of which by definition are ever-changing.

Because the notion of not-self seems so counterintuitive, the Buddha used some striking metaphors to help us understand this concept. One of the most familiar is a rainbow: when climatic conditions are right, we see a rainbow; when conditions change, it disappears. The same could be said for each of us. Once, in the Simile of the Lute (Samyutta Nikaya 246.9), he described a king who hears a lute playing for the first time and is "ravished," "enthralled," and "intoxicated" by the sound. The king asks his attendants to bring him the lute, but when he sees it, he insists that he wants only its sound. His men explain that the lute is many components:

"[It's] through the activity of numerous components that it sounds: that is, in dependence on the body, the skin, the neck, the frame, the strings, the bridge, and the appropriate human effort. Thus it is that this lute—made of numerous components, a great many components—sounds through the activity of numerous components."

Then the king would split the lute into ten pieces, a hundred pieces. Having split the lute into ten pieces, a hundred pieces, he would shave it to splinters. Having shaved it to splinters, he would burn it in a fire. Having burned it in a fire, he would reduce it to ashes. Having reduced it to ashes, he would winnow it before a high wind or let it be washed away by a swift-flowing stream. He would then say, "A sorry thing, this lute—whatever a lute may be—by which people have been so thoroughly tricked and deceived."

When first exposed to the notion of not-self, many people try to appeal to the existence of a soul. This is the type of situation when the Buddha used the metaphor of the heartwood of a banana tree (Samyutta Nikaya 95.3): "It's just as if a man going around wanting heartwood, seeking heartwood, searching for heartwood, would take a sharp ax and enter a forest. There he would see a large banana tree trunk: straight, young, without shoots. He would cut off the roof, cut off the crown, and unfurl the coil of the stem. There he wouldn't even find softwood, much less heartwood." The Buddha spoke often in similes to communicate difficult concepts to his followers. The man's hopeless search for the heartwood is as pointless as the king's searching for the music of a lute. Both are about the futility of seeking a soul or a self and complement each other. When we come to comprehend impermanence, concepts of "I am" and "my" and "mine" dissolve. We can experience the positive without clinging and the negative without aversion, both of which cause suffering. Simple to describe but not at all easy to do. Yet it is exactly attachment or aversion to what is impermanent—including ourselves—that is the source of suffering. The rest of the chapters in this book are about recognizing such attachments and how we can let go of them.

An extremely helpful mantra was offered by Bhikkhu Nanamoli to help us keep our awareness "steeped in the perception of inconstancy": "Whatever IS will be WAS."

Illness and Impermanence

Before the birth of Siddhartha, the Buddha-to-be, a seer foretold that he would become either a great political leader or a great spiritual leader. His father, Suddhodana, was head of the Sakya clan and wanted his son to follow in his footsteps rather than becoming a spiritual seeker. He did everything possible to shield his son from anything unpleasant that might distract him from the privileged life he was provided inside the palace. It is said that Suddhodana even had dead flowers pulled from plants on any route Siddhartha might take on an outing. Nevertheless, when Siddhartha was twenty-nine he had four encounters that affected him so profoundly that they are known as the heavenly messengers: For the first time, he saw a very old person, a very sick person, and a dead person; learning that these states would be his too caused him to come face to face with impermanence and ask himself what it means to be born in this human body. The fourth "messenger" was a holy man serenely walking the streets where Siddhartha had his earlier encounters. These unexpected meetings led him to forsake his life of luxury and sensual pleasures and to seek the answer to his question among ascetic spiritual practitioners.

Siddhartha's naiveté, his lack of understanding concerning aging, illness, and death until he was almost thirty, may seem unrealistic to us, but if we look at our own experiences in our privileged culture, many of us may find similarities. Unlike young children in developing countries who are surrounded by aging, illness, and death, most of us probably spent our youth encountering only transitory common childhood illnesses and shielded from extreme aging and death, except for perhaps the loss of a pet. Many of us reach adulthood before we experience or encounter serious illness.

If we have been blessed with good health but suddenly find ourselves facing a chronic or life-threatening illness, typically we react with shock, fear, and anger. Such moments can be transformative for us. At a gut level we experience our true impermanence, a stunning realization that can change forever how we see ourselves and our world. Realizing just how fragile and precious life is can make us treasure the blessings we have in the present; at the same time we see how futile it is to grasp our material world as if it, and we, would last forever. We can sense, too, our interconnectedness with all other beings because they, like us, will experience aging, illness, and death. Aging, illness, and death are the direct result of birth, eventually. They are inevitable for all of us; they are not personal. This universal truth can deeply move us to change the way we relate to

others. In one of the most beautiful verses of the *Dhammapada*, Thomas
Byrom renders the Buddha's teachings:

> In this world
> Hate never yet dispelled hate.
> Only love dispels hate.
> This is the law,
> Ancient and inexhaustible.
> You too shall pass away.
> Knowing this, how can you quarrel?

When we become seriously ill, even though we intellectually "know" all
these truths about impermanence and impersonality, it's hard not to just
plain feel bad—feel disappointed or angry at ourselves, sometimes even
feel embarrassed that "our bodies have let us down." I went through all
the emotions—positive and negative—when I became ill with a chronic,
life-threatening illness a decade ago. All the teachings have been helpful, but the single insight that has helped me the most (and others with
whom I've shared it) was something Vipassana teacher Sylvia Boorstein
said during a talk on karma: "My friend said, 'Whenever anyone asks me
how I am, I say I couldn't be better.'" Sylvia paused, then added, "That
statement is true for every one of us at every moment of our lives. If we
could be better, we would." This insight helped me to really comprehend
that I am a "moving river within a moving river" and that everything that
ever happened had to happen for me to be here, now, just as I am. This
realization was enormously relieving, and the mental suffering eased and
has never come back as intensely as it was, though I still live with the
physical illness. The Buddha put it this way: "The body is afflicted, weak,
and encumbered. For who, looking after this body, would claim even a
moment of true health, except through sheer foolishness? So you should
train yourself: 'Even though I may be afflicted in body, my mind will be
unafflicted.'"

Believe me, I know how challenging observing these teachings can
be. While working on this book, I was sorely tested to practice what I

preach: I had a freak accident involving my horse, which necessitated extensive surgery with plates, screws, rods, and, I suspect, soup spoons. After I had recovered enough to begin using a cane, I developed a condition known as compartment syndrome, requiring more surgery and almost amputation. I was back in a wheelchair and spent a seventh month in a hospital bed. I'm now back to a cane, doing water aerobics again, and am highly motivated to do intense physical therapy so I'll be able to ride my horse when summer comes. I'm not able-bodied, but I couldn't be better. Although we cannot control the illnesses that may afflict us, we can dissipate the mental anguish that accompanies them.

Practice and Reflection: Impermanence

1. Take a few moments to reflect on the impermanence of each of the "collectives": material form, feeling, perception, mental formations, consciousness. Explore briefly the impermanence of experience through each sense organ of your material form, noting that for each sense there is a specific consciousness, with memory, that enables us to recognize the object of that sense.

   • **Eye / vision / visual consciousness** occurs when the eye has contact with an object. Hold up one finger at arm's length away. Do you see it clearly, or is it blurred? Slowly move the finger closer to your eyes until it is about three inches away. Do you see it clearly, or is it blurred? When you go to bed at night, lie down on top of the covers, turn off the light, close then open your eyes, and look at your feet for one minute. Notice the adaptation of your eyes in the dark: at first you can't see your feet, then you can. Vision is constantly changing. Vision is not self.

- **Ear / hearing / hearing consciousness** occurs when the ears have contact with sound waves. Take a deep breath and expel the air forcefully. Notice that sound arises and then passes away. When a car drives past or an airplane flies overhead, notice that sound arises and then passes away, and that your hearing consciousness enables you to distinguish between the sound of a car and a plane. Has your hearing acuity changed as you have aged? Hearing is constantly changing. Hearing is not self.

- **Skin / touch / touch consciousness** occurs when inner or outer skin tissue has contact with an object. Take a deep breath through your nose and notice if there is a different perception of temperature in your nostrils when you inhale and exhale. Take a swallow of liquid and see how far you can perceive the sensation from your mouth into your throat. Touch your wrist or chest and feel your pulse or heartbeat, noticing that you can feel the change in pressure against your skin. After you've been in a bath or shower for a few minutes, do you ever turn on more or less hot water? Tactile sensations change constantly. Touch is not self.

- **Nose / smell / smell consciousness** occurs when the nose has contact with a scent. Put a small dab of a scented lotion below your nostrils on your upper lip and notice the strength of the perceived smell over the space of one minute. Strike a match, blow it out, hold it beneath your nose for a minute and notice the smell change. Then breathe through your mouth and see if the smell is still there. Scents constantly change. Perceiving smell is not self.

- **Tongue / taste / taste consciousness** occurs when the tongue has contact with a taste. Put a small dab of the scented lotion you used in the previous exercise on the end of your tongue and notice if it tastes the same as it smells; if you taste it primarily on the top, sides, or back of the tongue; if the taste lasts longer than the smell did; whether the taste is pleasant, unpleasant, or neutral. Think about your favorite food—its taste, texture, color—and see if there is any change to your taste organs, such as increased salivation. Do you enjoy any food as an adult that you didn't like as a child? Why? Taste is constantly changing. Tasting is not self.

- **Mind / mind consciousness** occurs when the mind has contact with mental formations such as emotions and thoughts. Bring to mind a pet or your closest friend, and notice over two or three minutes whether your thoughts are of the past, present, or future, and whether they are pleasant, unpleasant, or neutral. Bring to mind your least favorite politician or public personality, and notice over two or three minutes whether your thoughts are of the past, present, or future, and whether they are pleasant, unpleasant, or neutral. Remember an unsatisfying verbal exchange with another person and think of something you wish you had said. Mental formations are constantly changing. Mental formations are not self.

2. Reflect for a moment about how no aspect of our material form is permanent. This reflection may affect our perception of illness or pain.

   - If you have an illness or a pain or even a physical discomfort, bring your full awareness to the pain. What physical area comprises it? Is the pain the same everywhere you feel it? Do you experience the pain as pressure or heat or some other sensation?

- Recall that our material form is empty of a permanent separate self. Reflect that because of impermanence, the pain is not "your" pain but is merely present in your material form, which is impermanent.

- Try to relax into the pain and to breathe through it. Don't contract around the pain or try to bargain with it ("If I pay close enough attention, you'll go away"); this can make the pain more intense. As you breathe through it, reflect on the truth that the pain is present but is not you.

3.

Karma: Creating Suffering or Happiness

THE TERM *karma* has been so overused in popular culture that when most people encounter the word, they expect to hear about some unavoidable destiny, probably controlled by a mysterious force or being. In fact, our personal karma *is* controlled by a sometimes-mysterious being: ourselves.

The original Sanskrit term *karma* (*kamma* in Pali) literally means "action" or "deed"—*not* the fruit of that action. The "law of karma" is that all *intentional* actions have consequences. Nothing is ever lost—or, in the words of the venerable Vipassana teacher Ruth Denison, "Karma means you don't get away with nothin'." Also, karma can be created by individuals, families, and even nations, which makes some of the actions of groups and institutions rather ominous.

Causes and Conditions

Karma, like all our actions, is affected by both past and present factors. Occurrences in the natural, nonsentient world are not karma, because *karma* is defined as *volitional* action through body, speech, or mind. We thus are affected by many nonkarmic occurrences, such as weather, but karma may come into play because we put ourselves into the situation. For example, if lightning strikes a tree, this is not karma. However, if you choose to stand under a tree to get out of the rain, you may be struck by lightning as the karmic result of your actions. If through national policy—for another, broader example—we add to global warming and cause polar ice to melt, the resulting higher seas may flood our cities, making them uninhabitable.

An ideal metaphor for the way karma works is planting seeds. If you plant apple seeds, you'll eventually get apples, not asparagus. If the conditions are suitable—soil, moisture, temperature, sunlight—the seeds will germinate, sprouts will grow, and the plants will bear fruit. The physical environment has a critical role in what happens to the seed. If there is a drought, the seeds may not germinate the first season; the plants may be stunted when they do mature. Fertilized naturally or artificially, they may grow so wildly that they become dominant in their environment and crowd out other species. Some seeds, such as the lodgepole pine, require such a high temperature to germinate that they remain dormant until there is a forest fire. But when conditions are suitable, the seeds germinate and bear fruit—and so does karma.

For living beings, the result of karmic seeds may be physical or emotional. In geographical regions where there is war or oppression, children may be stunted physically or mentally because they have poor access to good nutrition. Everywhere, children may be damaged by drugs, disease, or environmental hazards encountered by their parents before the infants are even born. The physical world into which they are born can have great effect on them as they develop, and the emotional environment can contribute to whether they become warm and loving people or sociopaths.

Anyone who has chosen to share their life with pets has seen both the physical and the emotional effects that environment has. Before I learned better, I once bought a puppy that had come from a puppy mill. This puppy had all the physical characteristics of her breed, but she was a quite anxious little puppy and adult dog because she had been removed too young from her mother. She died unusually early from Cushing's syndrome, caused by generations of malnutrition in her puppy-mill lineage. I feel terrible that, by giving her breeder money, I may have helped to perpetuate suffering.

The person I am today has been created by the past karma of my nation, region, family, and own life. In each moment—if we are truly present for it—we have the choice of continuing to perpetuate everything that has led up to that moment or make decisions that will change our future karma. With mindfulness, we can make wise responses to the situations in our daily lives rather than mindlessly *re*acting—that is, acting out old karma.

Wearing Out Old Karma

If and only if we can be present within the now with mindfulness and understanding can we change our future karma. Mindfulness, supported by a commitment to living a life that doesn't harm ourselves or others, quite simply "wears out" old karma. When we consciously choose to act in a way that doesn't cause harm now or in the future, we change the course of our future karma. And it's never too late.

Note, however, that we can't change our past karma, and when we reap what we have sown in the past, it may not be particularly pleasant. As with all dis-ease, how we relate to it determines how much we suffer. Consider the example of a young woman who thought it was really cool to smoke cigarettes; trying to appear older, she started smoking when she was thirteen. When she was about forty—goaded by her children—she finally made the decision to stop smoking. So although she saved the cost of cigarettes, smelled better without smoke on her breath and clothes, and generally took up a healthier lifestyle, damage had been done to her lungs. The ill effects of her years of smoking left her with chronic obstructive pulmonary disease, and she became increasingly limited in what she could physically do. Rather than constantly complaining and asking, "Why me?" she acknowledged that she herself had caused her problem and became an advocate for helping others to stop smoking and hopefully avoid the discomforts and limitations she had.

Making New Karma

Recently a friend told me about an experience he'd just had. He had returned to the community where he lives one summer evening and was talking with friends. A mosquito landed on his arm. One friend reached over to swat it but was stopped by another who understands my friend's commitment to nonharming; this friend gently brushed the mosquito away. In this story there is a critically important dynamic in addition to the karmic implications.

Now, do this simple experiment: Hold out one arm and with the other hand slap your forearm. Now, still holding out that arm, use your other hand to lightly brush your forearm.

What is the difference between these two acts? *Intention.* In the first, you intended to slap your arm, so you turned your hand palm-down and did so. You did not consciously say to yourself, "Now I'm going to bend my elbow and raise my arm. Now I'm going to turn my hand and move it quickly downward." This was an action you had done before, you knew how to do it, and you could quickly and seemingly unconsciously just do it. Similarly, when you went to brush your arm, you didn't have to think through moving your arm or turning your hand. You already knew how to do it, and you just did it.

Nevertheless, the intention to move your hand in particular ways was there in your mind—whether you thought about it consciously or not—and you acted on each intention. There is in our minds an intention that precedes every thought, action, and word—and all too often we simply are "on automatic pilot," not in touch with our intentions.

As human beings who want to transform our everyday lives into spiritual practice, intention is the driving force in our success—or lack thereof. Wise intention is, as it says in Maurice Walsh's translation of Digha Nikaya 21, "The thought of renunciation, the thought of non-ill-will, the thought of harmlessness." It is critical that our intentions lead to words and speech that do not harm. The relationship between our intentions/thoughts and karma are clearly stated in the first verses of the *Dhammapada*, as rendered by Thomas Byrom:

> We are what we think.
> All that we are arises with our thoughts.

With our thoughts we make the world.
Speak or act with an impure mind
And trouble will follow you
As the wheel follows the ox that draws the cart.

We are what we think.
All that we are arises with our thoughts.
With our thoughts we make the world.
Speak or act with a pure mind
And happiness will follow you
As your shadow, unshakable.

These understandings are absolutely necessary if you are looking for a way to be mindful and to be happy. In Pali, the language in which this collection of the Buddha's verses was originally written, the same word—*citta*—is used for both "heart" and "mind." Thus, these verses illuminate the truth that wise thought/intention integrates reason and emotion, understanding and volition. Wise thought *is* wise intention, which does not harm.

The very good news the Buddha taught is that we can learn how to cultivate mindfulness and skillful qualities. We can transform our intentions to nonharming actions, bringing happiness to ourselves and those around us. We can even learn compassion for others who are creating unskillful karma for themselves. I observed an amazing example of compassion for others' karma a few years ago when the Dalai Lama offered a teaching in New York City to a large audience, many of whom had come from Taiwan for the teaching. As he often does, the Dalai Lama invited questions from the audience, and one person asked if the Dalai Lama didn't sometimes wish for vengeance against the Chinese who invaded Tibet. The Dalai Lama put his head down and began to weep. When he spoke again, he said, "Oh no. The Chinese are creating more bad karma for themselves than any pain they could cause the Tibetans." He was weeping for the karmic inheritance of those who had driven him from his homeland and were committing cultural genocide there.

Practice and Reflection: Karma

Take a few moments to reflect on karma:

- What physical image do you project through your choice of clothing and hair style? How do others respond to this image? Have you changed your image in the past twenty years? Thirty years?

- Recall one of your intentional actions of the past that today causes you shame, guilt, or remorse. Did you ever repeat that action after the first time? Why or why not?

- Recall something you said at some point in the past that you later regretted. Did you regret it at the time or only afterward? Did you say it intentionally?

- Have you unintentionally damaged a personal relationship through your own words or actions? Would you intentionally say or do the same thing again? Why or why not?

- Do you belong to the same political party as your parents? The same religion? Can you see where "family karma" is operating in any area of your life?

- Have any actions of our government—"national karma"— caused you dis-ease?

- For ten minutes, see if one of the questions above reveals a way you can cultivate mindfulness of your intentions in an area of your daily life.

4.
Cultivating Mindfulness

When I teach meditation classes, I begin by asking why people want to learn to meditate, what their expectations are, and—for more experienced practitioners—why they stay with the practice. Almost always the reasons for beginning meditation include stress reduction, a bliss trip, the need to change one's life. People who stay with meditation regularly report that they do so because "it works"; "I feel better when I meditate," they say, or "I feel like I'm coming home."

Trying to help my students pin down just what meditation is gets a bit trickier. Its simplest explanation is that meditation is the study of the mind; with practice, we can actually change the nature of the mind. Interestingly, the Buddha was meditating when he achieved enlightenment, but he didn't stop then. He continued to meditate for forty years after his enlightenment because he had learned that we can change—we can purify—our basic thoughts, actions, and ideals by continuously cultivating mindfulness.

The topic of meditation is often confusing because the term is used to mean so many different things: thought, deliberation, contemplation, reflection, even an altered state of consciousness. In this book, the term *meditation* is used for three specific and interrelated endeavors: concentration (*samadhi*, or single-pointed focus); insight (*vipassana*, or seeing things just as they really are); and mindfulness (*satipatthana*, or full awareness in the body and mind of what is happening).

Many formal courses in meditation begin with concentration, then expand to insight, and finally address mindfulness. Though, in fact, it is virtually impossible to do any single form without the others creeping in. Here we'll first look briefly at concentration and insight, and then focus on mindfulness—which is the most critical aspect of meditation for making our lives into spiritual practice.

As I learned more about mindfulness, I came to understand increasingly how absolutely necessary it is to spiritual practice. Perhaps because mindfulness is in the present moment, in the now, which is the only time that is "real," the only moment where we have the choices that affect our future lives. Also, being mindful in the present moment enriches our lives greatly, as we'll see at the end of this chapter when we explore mindful eating. As meditation teacher Jack Kornfield likes to say, quoting a sign in a Las Vegas casino: "You must be present to win."

The Basics of Meditation

The most important thing for a beginner on the path to spiritual freedom is to make the decision to establish a daily meditation practice, even if only for a few minutes, at a regular time and place. The goal is to find a quiet spot where you will not be interrupted. If it is possible to choose a place in your home where you can regularly meditate, perhaps with a small altar there, that is ideal. If not, you can learn a lesson from the Dalai Lama, who when he travels frequently meditates sitting in the center of the bed in his hotel room.

There's nothing magic about sitting in a position like a pretzel on the floor. This posture has been favored for millennia by people who were raised in cultures where they sat frequently in a cross-legged posture throughout their lives. There is one advantage to sitting this way: it is very stable, and if you can build up your flexibility enough to sit cross-legged, the perception of balance and stability can enhance your practice. In fact, there are four positions for meditation: sitting, standing, lying down, and walking. If you can think of any others, they'd be fine too. One option, if you need back support, is to fold a blanket several times to be a "mat" on the floor and then to fold over a pillow to be your "cushion," which you position against the side of the bed so that you lean on it. As the population that ardently embraced meditation in the West has aged, many practitioners—including some teachers—have chosen to sit in a chair to meditate. Whatever posture you choose, find one where you can sit still—erect and alert but not rigid—for as long as you plan your meditation session to be.

Concentration Meditation

Basic concentration practice is one-pointed focus on an object. The breath as the object of contemplation is ideal; it's free, and it's always available. Most importantly, when you focus your attention on your breath, you become immersed in your body, with immediate access to body, feelings, mind, and mind-objects.

Here are basic instructions for concentration meditation:

- Let your eyes gently close. Rest your hands on your lap or thighs, or clasp them loosely just below your waist, in front of and against your abdomen.
- Sitting comfortably, take several deep breaths, then let your breath return to normal and do not control the length or depth of each breath.
- Identify where you feel your breath most strongly: perhaps the upper lip or nostrils, or perhaps the abdomen, slightly below the navel.
- Keenly observe the details and subtleties of your breath at this focal spot. Is your breath long or short? Is it deep or shallow? Is it coarse or smooth? Is it cooler on an inhalation than on an exhalation? Is there a space between your inhalation and exhalation? Is it longer or shorter between your exhalation and inhalation?
- As soon as you realize that your attention has wandered—and it will—bring your awareness back to your breath.

In the same way, you can begin using the breath to achieve stillness and balance, and to focus on any feelings of pleasant, unpleasant, or neutral that come up. With practice, you also can become aware of activity of the mind and of thoughts and emotions. But just as you let the sensations of the breath arise and pass away, so too do your perceptions of other frames of reference, such as sounds, arise and pass away, without your becoming attached to them, in what Thanissaro Bhikkhu refers to as "choiceless awareness." These arisings and passings away are the heart of insight and mindfulness practice.

Some Tips

- When you first begin to meditate, you may find that you can't keep your attention steady for longer than a breath or two. There are two techniques that can help:
  1. Count breaths: in and out is 1, then in and out is 2, etc. When your attention wanders, go back to 1.
  2. Use "noting"—that is, an internal whisper noting what's happening: "in," "out," "in," "out," "thinking," "thinking," "in," "out"...

  As soon as your attention has become steadier—either in your overall practice or in a given sitting—let your attention go directly to your breathing without these cues.
- When you realize that your mind has wandered away, don't beat yourself up for your lack of concentration. Instead, celebrate the moment you come back to your breath with the happy realization framed by meditation teacher Eric Kolvig's exclamation: "Hooray! I'm back!" These moments of coming into the now are moments of insight.
- If you are experiencing particularly disturbing thoughts or emotions, try doing walking meditation: Using your feet as the focus of your attention, put all your weight on your left foot; roll your right foot onto its toe, lift that foot, move it forward, place it; shift your weight to your right foot as your left foot rolls to the toe, you lift that foot, move it, place it, shift your weight, etc. Using noting for the segments of walking meditation can be helpful, as can walking outdoors if a

quiet place is available. When you do walking meditation, the goal is to keep your attention steady on lifting the foot, moving the foot, placing the foot, and shifting the weight. You're not going anywhere. You're not learning how to walk any more than you're learning how to breathe when you focus on your breath.

Besides the breath and the feet, it is possible to use other internal and external objects of attention, including words, as we'll see in chapter 14. No matter what your object, meditation practice will bring you the stillness of mind that will enable you to be alert and present in the moment and thus able to strengthen your concentration and mindfulness. Meditation practice is the expression of the intention to develop mindfulness and is thus the link between karma and the purification of our actions that is expressed through the personal ideals explored in part II. But in the way are the five hindrances.

The Five Hindrances

In meditation and in life there are five conditions known as the hindrances that can derail our concentration and even our intentions. A popular image of the Buddha shows him seated cross-legged on a lotus blossom, the fingers of his right hand pointed downward, touching the earth. Such images depict one encounter between the Buddha and Mara, the Evil One—sometimes interpreted as the negative psychological factors in each of us, sometimes as an actual malevolent deity—who pursued the Buddha, challenging his enlightenment from the night it occurred. In this particular depiction, Mara has asked just who the Buddha thinks he is to claim enlightenment; Mara tries to seed doubt in the Buddha's mind. When the Buddha reached down to touch the earth, he invoked the earth to witness his right to liberation.

Each time we meditate we reenact the Buddha's experiences, complete with our own personal Maras, the five hindrances: desire, aversion, sloth and torpor, restlessness, and doubt.

1. **Desire/sensuality/greed.** We tend to think of sensual desire as having to do with the physical senses, but the mind is considered a sense organ in Buddhism, and desire for objects of the mind can be a powerful hindrance in the same way that lust for, say, sexual experience can be. Just as we may cling to the notion that a particular partner, job, car, or sense experience can make us permanently happy, so too may we feel that if we could just have a blissful meditation experience, for instance, we'd be happy. When we're sitting, desire might interfere with our meditation in the form of a yearning for the "ideal" meditation experience, for the bell ending the session, for pizza or ice cream, or for a liaison with the attractive person sitting near us. What our minds seem to envision as happiness is an endless parade of great meals, good sex, business successes, solved Sudokus, equanimous meditations. But of course the parade is not endless—even as we hold on to one sense experience it passes away, and no two meditation sessions are ever alike.

    One way to contemplate the impermanence of sensual desire is to clearly separate the desire from its object and to envision its object as changing and putrefying. The aspect of desire expressed as greed can be contemplated by considering what happens with overindulgence in food and alcohol; in fact some teachers insist that moderation in eating is an ideal way to cultivate nongreed. A striking metaphor for overindulgence due to greed are some of the current ads for "male enhancement" that seem to promise total lasting happiness but caution that if you have an erection lasting for four hours, you should go to the hospital or call 911. Nothing really lasts, so you may have created a crisis in your search for lasting happiness—but if it does last, please call 911.

    Contemplation of impermanence is the antidote to clinging.

2. **Aversion/hatred/ill-will:** Just as desire causes us to grasp its object, aversion causes us to push that object away. As with desire, it is helpful to separate the aversive feelings from their object and to realize that both are impermanent. If the object of the aversion during med-

itation is, for example, a pain in the knee, we tend to concentrate on it so strongly that we cause physical contraction, which can intensify the pain and the aversion. When we can examine the nature of the pain, we can often relax into it and it passes (if you ever get a painful cramp in the arch of your foot while sitting, do this and you'll be surprised at how quickly the pain dissipates). Very often our aversion is directed to other beings and takes forms such as anger, jealousy, and blame. For such aversion the antidote is love—in the sense of metta, loving-kindness, explored deeply in chapter 14.

3. **Sloth and torpor / sleepiness:** Sometimes when we close our eyes to meditate, we may feel overwhelmed by sleepiness. In some cases, we have been leading a very stressful life and simply relaxing makes us sink into sleepiness. Sometimes we've just eaten a full meal, and oxygen is anywhere except in the brain. Sometimes we truly are sleep-deprived. Whatever the case, the mind seems to say, "There's nothing happening. Time to sleep." The trick is to raise our energy level enough to dispel the lethargy. One way to do this is to hold to an alert posture. Opening our eyes and contemplating light can help. If you feel as if you're on the edge of falling asleep, stand up and continue meditating. Other ways to overcome sleepiness can be to go for a vigorous walk, splash the face with cold water, and—according to the Buddha— pull on the earlobes as part of your meditation when you are fighting fatigue. The natural antidote for sloth and torpor is wise effort, which we'll discuss in chapter 10.

4. **Restlessness:** This hindrance can take a physical form, such as agitation, or a mental form, such as worrying or compulsive planning. A first step in dealing with restlessness while meditating is to put more energy into concentration on the movement of the breath. A frequently invoked metaphor for training the mind is taming an elephant: We must train the elephant before it can do useful work, so we tie it to a post; at first it snorts and stomps and pulls against the rope, but eventually it

settles down. Our minds are the same way, and restlessness is the way the mind rebels against being trained through single-pointed concentration. Eventually, when we repeatedly bring our attention back to the breath, when we insist on tying it to the post, the mind will settle down. Sometimes when the mental restlessness takes the form of worry, we can contemplate the Dharma, especially teachings on impermanence and the insubstantiality of worry and other mental formations.

5. **Doubt**: In many ways doubt is the most insidious of the hindrances; it seems so reasonable, and it is self-generated and self-sustained. When we are sitting, doubt often takes the form of thoughts such as "This is the wrong practice for me," "This is the wrong teacher for me," "I'm too physically frail to expect myself to be able to sit for so long." If you can recognize doubt for what it is, just acknowledge it by noting "Doubt, doubt." But if doubt is persistent, it's very important to talk about these thoughts with a teacher or a spiritual friend experienced with meditation practice.

During meditation, our tasks in relationship to the hindrances are expressions of wise effort: we must realize that a hindrance is present or absent, identify it, let go of any hindrance present, and guard against the arising of any hindrance not present. For those who don't want to train the elephant, one verse of the the *Dhammapada*, as translated by Thanissaro Bhikkhu, shows dramatically what the hindrances out of control can do to our minds:

> Like a fish
> pulled from its home in the water
> & thrown on land:
> this mind flips & flaps about
> to escape Mara's sway.

> Hard to hold down,
> nimble

alighting wherever it likes:
> the mind.
> Its taming is good.
> The mind well-tamed
>> brings ease.

Attentiveness to the hindrances during meditation is extremely helpful in seeing them when they manifest in our daily lives.

Frames of Reference

One the most crucial and complex teachings of the Buddha can be called the Four Frames of Reference (or the Four Foundations) for Mindfulness. These four frames of reference are the body, feelings, the mind, and mental formations; awareness of them is the key to the transformation of the personal ideals that we seek. In Bhikkhu Bodhi's translation of Majjhima Nikaya 10.2, the Buddha stressed the importance of the four frames of reference:

> This is the direct path for the purification of beings, for the surmounting of sorrow and lamentation, for the disappearance of pain and grief, for the attainment of the true way.

With ardent effort we immerse our mindfulness in the body and contemplate the body just as it is—young, old, comfortable, uncomfortable—without any reference to the outside world or any greed, aversion, or delusion that the body be otherwise; without anything that may distract us. We also immerse our mindfulness in feelings as feelings, discerning them as pleasant, unpleasant, or neutral with bare attention, without stories, without judgment relative to the outside world.

Similarly, we contemplate the mind and mental formations. Insight Meditation Society founder Joseph Goldstein quotes his teacher: "If you want to know the nature of mind, sit down and watch it." When we do contemplate mind as mind without distraction, we can achieve the balance and stability that enable us to perceive causality and mind-objects such as emotions and thoughts as they arise and pass away, which gives rise to insight and lets us see reality as it is.

All of this seems straightforward, simple—and it is—but it is not easy, because our efforts at mindfulness are beset by the five hindrances. It simply is not possible to be mindful when a hindrance is present.

❖ Thousands of volumes about the Four Frames of Reference for Mindfulness have been written. It is interesting to read them—but it is also possible to experience the basics in the following short exercise. Note: Do not do this exercise if you have cardiac or respiratory problems and stop it immediately if you experience strong distress.

Repeat the following three times:

1. Take three normal breaths.
2. Inhale deeply, deeply; keep inhaling after you think you can't take in any more air.
3. Exhale slowly, slowly, and continue to exhale even if you feel there is no more air to squeeze out.
4. Take three normal breaths.

Here's what happens in terms of the frames of reference:

1. body awareness
2. body awareness, unpleasant feelings, mind states such as anxiety, aversive thoughts about this exercise or instructions or self
3. body awareness, unpleasant feelings, mind states such as anxiety, aversive thoughts about this exercise or instructions or even self
4. body awareness

❖ There's a much more pleasant way to experience mindfulness that I use whenever I teach a brand-new group of meditation students. Whether they are youthful attendees at a center or elders in a retirement community, I begin the classes the same way, with a guided meditation of eating a tangerine (or kiwi or whatever fruit is seasonal). At the end, I ask the students about their experience and regularly hear comments like "Where'd you find *those* tangerines?" "The taste exploded in my mouth!" and "I don't think I ever really ate a tangerine before!" I then tell everyone that they've just had their first mindfulness meditation and that all the experiences of their lives can be just as intense if they cultivate mindfulness and have a lot of stamina. So join me in this meditation on eating a tangerine or a kiwi or trail mix, or anything you like.

1. Sit comfortably with your eyes closed for a few minutes, holding a tangerine in your hand.
2. With your eyes closed, get a tactile sense of the tangerine—its shape, texture, temperature.
3. Open your eyes and look carefully at the tangerine. Is its color even overall, or are some parts a different color or even mottled?
4. Smell the tangerine. How strong is the odor? Is it familiar or unfamiliar?
5. Peel the tangerine and examine the peel. What is the difference in color between the inside and the outside? In the texture? In the smell? Bite into the skin and notice the taste.
6. Hold the peeled fruit and examine it. Is the flesh darker or lighter than the peel? Are the white "webs" on the skin holding the flesh darker or lighter than the outside of the peel? Than the inside of the peel?
7. How many sections are there? Are the divisions symmetrical?
8. Break apart the sections. Can you see any seeds through the translucent skin of each section? Is there a seed for each section?
9. Hold one section in your hand and smell it. Does it smell like the outside of the tangerine before you peeled it?
10. Do you notice any change inside your mouth when you smell the tangerine?
11. Place that one section of tangerine into your mouth but do not chew. What is happening inside your mouth? Are you salivating? Do you experience a desire to chew the fruit?
12. Close your eyes. Begin to slowly chew that section of tangerine, but do not swallow. What is happening inside your mouth? Are you

salivating? As you chew does your tongue move around? Where do you taste the tangerine most strongly—on the front or back, sides, or middle of your tongue?

13. When you have thoroughly chewed the fruit, swallow it and see how far you can feel it travel down your throat.

14. Open your eyes, choose another section of fruit, and eat it mindfully, in the same way, until you've finished the tangerine. Has your opinion of eating tangerines changed?

15. Describe this experience to a friend in as much detail as you can, or use your description as a free-writing exercise.

One very pleasant way to incorporate mindfulness into your daily life is mindfully to eat the first ten bites of a meal—or a whole meal, if your life situation makes this possible.

Practice and Reflection: The Hindrances

1. Practice sitting meditation for thirty minutes. Observe the arising and passing away of the hindrances.

- Was one hindrance predominant or did you have a multiple-hindrance attack?

- Did you experience any of the hindrances as pleasant? Which ones?

- How long were you aware of a hindrance before it dissipated?

2. Do walking meditation for ten minutes. Observe the arising and passing away of the hindrances.

- Was one hindrance predominant or did you have a multiple-hindrance attack?

- Did you experience any of the hindrances as pleasant? Which ones?

- How long were you aware of a hindrance before it dissipated?

- Were the hindrances present more strongly when you were sitting or when you were walking?

3. Write down a list of the hindrances and several examples of how each one most frequently arises when you're not on the cushion. Some examples:

- Desire: to eat between meals, to telephone a friend, to buy new clothes.

- Aversion: to doing the dishes, to watching sitcoms or some other kind of television program, to hearing loud cars or motorcycles go by.

- Restlessness: getting up and moving around during the day, repeatedly planning the same trip (to the grocery store or a vacation), feeling anxiety about meeting new people.

- Sloth and torpor: not wanting to get up in the morning, wanting to take a nap during the day, feeling bored, procrastinating.

- Doubt: Not wanting to continue with a meditation practice, questioning whether you are up to the life or job you have, feeling that you need to make new, different friends.

4. Consider this list of hindrances in daily life. See if strategies for dealing with them emerge. Can you transfer these strategies to your meditation practice?

5. Begin to cultivate mindfulness in your everyday life:

- Select one activity such as eating, brushing or flossing your teeth, bathing yourself, opening a door, putting your hands in water, going up or down stairs.

- Each time you do this activity make an effort to be fully, mindfully present for it.

- In a week or so, when you are consistently mindful during that activity, add a second one. Later, a third one, etc.

- Observe what happens to your mindfulness during one of these activities if you engage in conversation at the same time. See if—for even a short time—you can be mindful during speech.

Part II
Life Practice: Our Personal Ideals

5.
An Introduction to the Perfections

AS A YOUNG CHILD, I loved to play with something called "magic seeds." I'd drop them into a glass of water, and they would suddenly swell into huge and exotic paper flowers, filling me with wonder and joy. I sometimes wish that heart characteristics like generosity and patience were like that and would suddenly bloom into full flower the moment I plant the seeds. But they don't. They must be carefully cultivated.

The word *paramis* (Pali), or *paramitas* (Sanskrit), is usually translated as "perfections," but the literal derivation is "that which has been completed." This definition is fascinating—and reassuring—in that it implies that all of these characteristics are natural qualities of the heart that we can develop, that we can perfect. With practice, they can be completed.

The Buddha taught that we can learn to express these heart characteristics; by example, he showed that we could perfect them. And throughout his teachings he gives us quite clear instructions about how to do so. Scholars and the Buddha himself also used the fascinating device of the Jataka Tales: stories that show the Buddha in his previous lifetimes and demonstrate that he could perfect these heart ideals under the most challenging conditions, while he was an animal or even a tree. The lesson is clear: if he could do it, we can do it.

The perfections are ten specific ways of benefiting other beings—when they are undertaken with mindfulness, compassion, and skillful means, when they are cultivated with the aspiration for liberation for oneself and all beings. The opposites of all perfections are greed, hatred, and delusion. Additionally striking: the perfections are not specifically Buddhist. These "sacred adornments of the heart" are found historically among people of good will everywhere on our planet.

Early scholars during the centuries after the Buddha's death tried to identify the characteristics of the heart-mind that, when perfected, were the foundation for his buddhahood. They often looked back over thousands of years of stories, some of which are even older than any known historical buddha. The earliest-known extant work on these ideals is believed to be the *Treatise on the Paramis*, written by the fifth-century scholar-monk Acariya Dhammapala. A later work, *A Guide to the Bodhisattva's Way of Life*, by the eighth-century northern Indian scholar-monk Shantideva, is still used as a popular teaching text by the Dalai Lama and other Tibetan Buddhist teachers.

Dhammapala gives several explanations for the sequence of the perfections. In one, each quality is strengthened by the cultivation of the one that follows it. In another, the quality is "purified" by the one that follows. The sequence has much to do with the order in which the perfections are traditionally taught, but it also has much to do with the way the Buddha integrated them throughout his teachings—for example, when he went into a new community his first talk was always about generosity, the first perfection.

Here are the perfections, in order, with some key factors and characteristics, according to Dhammapala:

1. **Generosity** is believed to be common to all beings and to be the easiest of the perfections to practice, so one begins with it. Its chief characteristic is the relinquishing of greed, craving, and attachment.
2. **Ethical Integrity, or Morality or Virtue,** follows generosity because it purifies both the giver and the receiver, and its goal is to dispel unskillful behavior and to manifest as purity of virtue.
3. **Renunciation, or Letting Go,** perfects morality by retreating from sense pleasures and by confirming the ultimate unsatisfactoriness of sense pleasures.

4. **Wisdom** perfects and purifies renunciation because it penetrates and illuminates the true, empty nature of all phenomena.

5. **Wise Effort** perfects wisdom by arousing the energy to apply it and to create a sense of spiritual urgency.

6. **Patience** perfects wise effort, by sustaining our efforts in the face of suffering and craving.

7. **Truthfulness** strengthens patience and enables one to use skillful speech and to validate the reality of phenomena.

8. **Resolve, or Determination,** perfects truthfulness by strengthening unshakable commitment to enlightenment.

9. **Loving-Kindness** perfects resolve by ensuring that it is put in the service of skillful tasks for the benefit of other beings.

10. **Equanimity** perfects loving-kindness by ensuring impartiality toward all beings in recognition that they are the heirs of their own karma.

The mastery of *all* of these sacred ideals is perfect liberation, living our whole lives as spiritual practice.

Practice and Reflection: The Perfections

1. Reflect briefly on what each perfection means to you.

2. Does any one perfection seem more important to you than the others? Which one? Why?

3. If you could add one or two other qualities of the heart to this list of perfections, what would they be?

6.

Generosity

Resolution: May my heart be open to give and to receive with joy and ease.

Mantra: May I give with joy.

How DO WE CULTIVATE a generous heart that is spontaneous, joyous, naturally at ease?

There's a great difference between the simple act of giving and generosity. True generosity is motivated by a desire to benefit all beings, which makes generosity a perfection, a sign of spiritual maturity. But is generosity a natural quality of the heart?

A notable story about the Buddha and generosity describes his return to his hometown for the first time after his enlightenment. Because the Buddha had not yet come to his own home, his father went around town, looking for him. When he found his son, he was accepting a potato from a poor woman in tattered clothes. Later, his father chided the Buddha about begging at such a poor shack instead of coming first to his home to eat. According to Vietnamese monk Thich Nhat Hanh, the Buddha replied, "Father, begging is a spiritual practice which helps [me] develop humility and see that all persons are equal. When I receive a small potato from a poor family, it is no different than when I receive an elegant dish served by a king... Everyone, no matter how poor he is, can attain liberation and enlightenment. Begging does not demean my own dignity. It recognizes the inherent dignity of all persons."

The striking lessons in this story are that we should not deny anyone—rich or poor—the opportunity to be generous, that anyone can attain liberation, and that generosity is the human starting point. Generosity is a basic constituent in all major religions, as Mahatma Gandhi noted when he said that "gentleness, self-sacrifice, and generosity are the exclusive possession of no one race or religion." Stories of Good Samaritans and Secret Santas abound. We grow up being told that it's better to give than to receive. Strangers smile as they hold doors open for us.

Every day presents us with many opportunities for generosity. When I reflect on the teaching that we should not deny anyone—rich or poor—the opportunity for generosity, I often recall the most generous act I've personally witnessed. Some years ago I went as a volunteer into a women's shelter in lower Manhattan to try to carry a message of hope. The women were dressed in ragged clothes. They were not clean and clearly had recently come into the shelter from living on the Bowery. Many of the women had repeatedly been inmates of mental institutions who had been turned out because of a belief that modern medications would keep them stable. The women had stopped their medications very soon after release, had become disoriented, and soon were living on the streets again.

After several hours, when I was getting ready to leave the shelter, one of the women, who had seemed quite delusional during our session, came up to me and said hesitatingly, "I want to give you a present."

"Thank you," I replied.

She reached into a pocket of her shirt and pulled out a folded piece of foil, a chewing gum wrapper. Holding it out to me, she met my eyes and said, "When the Pope was here, I held this up and he blessed it. I want you to have it." We made a penetrating connection and both became misty-eyed.

Generosity First

When early scholars began the list of the perfections with generosity, they did so as a reflection of the way the Buddha offered his teachings. Numerous discourses record that the Buddha's first talk in a new community was often about generosity. When I first read this, I just assumed he wanted to make sure that he and his followers got enough to eat. Wrong. Generosity is a foundational building block of spiritual development. Perhaps the Buddha began with generosity because it is and has been so widely accepted as one of the most basic human virtues by so many cultures.

In any case, when the Buddha went into a new community, he regularly used a particular sequence of teachings: he began with a talk about generosity, then spoke about morality, then about karma, then about the benefits of renunciation. When he felt that his listeners had understood all these teachings, only then would he give his first talk on suffering, its cause, and its end. He would explain that a universal condition of life is stress or suffering (*dukkha* in Pali and Sanskrit), and that the cause of suffering is clinging or attachment. Therefore, the end of suffering is nonclinging or nonattachment, and the path to liberation begins with generosity, the natural antidote to greed or clinging. The great value of generosity would become clear.

Clinging or attachment—the source of suffering—cannot exist at the same time as true generosity. By cultivating generosity, we can bring an end to clinging, an end to attachment to stinginess, to material things, even to our most cherished ideas and sense of self.

Many volumes have been written about the Buddha's teachings on generosity, but one strong cluster of teachings focuses on the way we can practice generosity: (1) By relinquishing external or material things—including one's belongings and even body and life—to benefit others; (2) by giving others the gift of freedom from fear; and (3) by giving others the Dharma: a complex term with many meanings, including natural law, truth, the Buddha's specific teachings, and each moment's experience. We'll discuss each of these three, one by one.

Giving Material Things

Most of us think of generosity as giving material things—perhaps taking clothes we no longer want to a thrift shop or making charitable contributions—but it encompasses so much more. We *are* urged to give our possessions to those in need: land, gold, cattle, children, spouses, even body parts, and our lives themselves. Because so many villagers were new to his teachings, and some were quite young, the Buddha often relied on Jataka Tales, those fables about his previous lives, to make his points about generosity.

In one dramatic tale, the deva Sakka (in early cosmology, a celestial being who lives in a fortunate realm) came into a forest disguised as a famished nobleman to test, in turn, the virtue of an otter, a jackal, a monkey, and a hare. The first three had fish, mangoes, and other foods to offer, according to their spiritual precepts, to anyone who asked. But the nobleman refused these gifts each time and said this for him was a day of fasting, and he told each of them he would come back the next day. Finally the nobleman came to the hare, who had nothing to offer except inedible (to humans) grass. The hare was so filled with shame at being unable to meet his spiritual responsibility that he threw himself upon burning coals in order to give the nobleman his roasted flesh, without causing the nobleman himself the bad karma of having to take a life in order to eat. But miraculously the fire did not burn the hare at all, and Sakka revealed his true identity. Telling the hare that his virtue would be known for eons, he painted the moon with the face of a hare. I never was able to see "the man in the moon," but sometimes there seems to be the ephemeral face of a hare.

In many parts of especially Southeast Asia, traditions of generosity by offering food have been nurtured for centuries. It is common in small and often poor villages to see adults and children lining the road each morning with bowls of food. When monks with begging bowls arrive, they are each given a small portion of rice or other food, often ladled by the children, who grow up with this example of generosity as a natural part of their culture.

Few of us will be called upon to give up our lives as acts of generosity, but some, especially those serving in the military, as police officers, or as firefighters may make this kind of sacrifice. We certainly saw this phenomenon after the 9/11 plane bombings when uniformed public servants, medical people, and just plain ordinary citizens rushed to the

World Trade Center to try to help victims. Similarly, many "civilian" onlookers and participants were the first responders in the 2013 Boston Marathon bombing. We also hear of family members who lose their lives trying to save a child, and there are numerous reports of total strangers who undergo surgery to donate an organ to someone in need.

None of this means that we, as householders, must give away so many material possessions as to be irresponsible and not meet our personal obligations. The Buddha often gave very specific instructions on our responsibilities to our families and friends. But he also spoke of the value of giving to suppliants who ask of us something that we have and can relinquish.

Can we cultivate generosity if there is no one to give to? The fifth-century monk Dhammapala, in his *Treatise on the Paramis*, asks, "If there were no suppliants, how would I fulfill the perfection of giving?" This question is Dhammapala's way of telling us that we find lessons for our spiritual life among even the most unexpected "teachers" if we are open to and mindful of our everyday experiences.

I once had a quite revealing experience with suppliants, through which I learned a valuable lesson concerning the attitude and motivations for giving. I had always thought of myself as a generous person, but there came a day when I realized that my generosity was conditional. I was talking with a Zen teacher about generosity, and she said that generosity should be as natural and spontaneous as "fluffing up your pillow in your sleep." Mine wasn't.

I was living in New York City at the time and walked about a half-hour each way to work. I passed many suppliants—homeless people and panhandlers—who always asked for money for food. In my mind, I was sure they'd use my money for booze or drugs, and I was not about to contribute to their downfall, though I don't know what they could have bought with my quarter. One day someone broke through my armor; a man said to me, "I'm so hungry. Please give me some money so I can eat." I went into a deli, bought him coffee and breakfast, and gave it to him. He threw it at me. "You see?" I said to myself, and that was the end of my generosity to suppliants on the street for a while.

After the Zen teacher's lesson, I began to buy a bunch of bananas from a street vendor by my office and give them to any people on my walk home who said they were hungry. Then I started also carrying quarters in one pocket to give to people. Finally dollar bills. It was slow, but I began to learn how to cultivate generosity that included spontaneity—that didn't judge, that didn't second-guess.

Many organizations give so much help to so many people in need. Consider giving donations to institutions in friends' names as gifts. Giving such gifts is "catching"—the recipients often then make similar gifts to others, or to us. I have received very few material gifts in recent years, but one friend over the years has consistently given me part of a water buffalo through Heifer International—an organization working to end hunger and poverty by donating livestock to struggling communities. This kind of giving is one of the ways we can practice the synthesizing of generosity and wisdom.

Giving the Gift of Fearlessness

The second of the great gifts we can give to others is freedom from fear.

Many of the gifts of money or goods or time we offer may do much to relieve fear in another's life. But there are other ways to give that gift. If you are reading this book, you are probably already inclined to give the gift of freedom from fear. Each time you resolve to not harm another being, you give that gift.

For laypeople, this gift has been codified in Buddhism as the five precepts, which are about one thing only—nonharming, through action, through not taking what is not given, through avoiding sexual misconduct, through speech, and through not misusing mind-altering substances. Chapter 7 will look at the five precepts in detail, but a few points about them are worth iterating here. They're not commandments or orders but rather are "training guidelines" by which householders can learn to cause themselves and others minimal suffering. These are everyday actions or common practices that enlightened beings would agree are not harmful—such as a parent who gives up smoking cigarettes so his newborn child won't be exposed to secondhand smoke, or a grand-parent who gets hearing aids so that her family can speak at a normal volume around her, or family members who take short showers to conserve water.

Giving the gift of fearlessness is the primary example of the synthesizing of generosity and virtue. Like all generosity, it is characterized by relinquishing greed, craving, and attachment.

Giving Truth

The Buddha repeatedly said that giving truth is practicing the highest kind of generosity.

A gift of truth may be either material or immaterial. For instance, one can give a material gift of truth by giving a friend a book of wise teachings for his or her birthday. Or one can give an immaterial gift of truth by demonstrating a wise and compassionate way to live. A Christian saying is that "I may be the only Bible some people read." The mindfulness, wisdom, and compassion we develop through our meditation practice are observed by others around us, even if we never quote a psalm or sutra to them. A few of us may have the opportunity to teach or to write about these truths, but all of us have the opportunity to try to cultivate in our daily lives sacred ideals and virtues, and through this, we all become teachers. We teach by walking the talk. A few examples:

- When I first make donations in other people's names, they often ask me about it, or at least give me the opportunity to say something like "Everyone I know has so many things, and this is a way to honor my friends by giving something truly needed."
- When people see me catch an insect and take it outside, they sometimes say, "Why don't you just swat it?" I reply, "It just doesn't feel good to kill things, even bugs."
- When someone says, "Why don't you have air conditioning?" I reply, "In this climate the overhead fan works really well and uses much less energy than air conditioning."

- When people in a spiritual discussion raise a question, I thank them for giving everyone there another opportunity for reflection.
- Accessibility for people with physical limitations is sometimes very difficult, so it's important—especially among our aging population—to actively look for ways to assist: hold a door open, get an item down from a high store shelf, or insist that public spaces have ramps, accessible bathrooms, etc.

When they see how I respond to situations like these, people often say, "Oh, I never thought of it that way."

There's a lovely custom in some Asian Buddhist communities: When laypeople offer food, robes, or medicine to monks, the monks chant blessings. At the same time, the laypeople pour water over their own hands to symbolize a river filling the ocean, showing that this deed is done for the benefit of all beings.

Practice and Reflection: Generosity

1. Let your eyes close gently, and reflect on these questions about generosity.

   - Do you consider yourself a generous person? What does "generous person" mean to you?

   - Do you feel needy when you have acted generously? How do you feel?

2. Reflect on giving material things:

   - Have you made "emergency" donations to victims of natural disasters such as a tsunami in south Asia, an earthquake in Pakistan, a mudslide in Central America, or a tornado or ecological catastrophe in the United States? Did the geographical location of the disaster affect whether or not you made a donation?

- Have you spontaneously given to suppliants who have approached you in person, such as panhandlers?

- If a friend asks you for a favor, do you stop and judge it before responding?

- Do you give donations in others' names as gifts? Why or why not?

3. Reflect on giving the gift of fearlessness:

- By practicing nonharming, do you give the gift of safety to those in your family? Your community? Your nation? Your planet?

- Do you have the generosity of "good manners"—letting others go ahead of you in a line, letting cars merge easily, holding doors for others, being pleasant to service people when you interact with them, and giving genuine attention to someone who is trying to tell you something?

- Are there beings—individuals, groups, religions, nations —for whom you would willingly risk or sacrifice your life? Do you consider it generosity when any others, such as firefighters, do? How about suicide bombers?

4. Can you make the resolve to cultivate a heart that remains open to give and receive easily and with joy? List some specific ways you can cultivate generosity in your daily life.

5. Sit quietly for ten minutes and do a meditation practice using the repetition of these phrases as the object of your concentration/mindfulness. As you silently repeat the phrases, do so slowly enough to feel what each one would be like in your life:

> May I be happy.
> May I be healthy.
> May I live in safety.
> May I give with joy.

7.
Ethical Integrity

Resolution: May ethical integrity in thoughts, words, and
actions be my gift to myself and the beings
around me.

Mantra: May I give freedom from fear to all beings.

ETHICAL INTEGRITY, MORALITY, VIRTUE—all are liberating qualities
of the heart-mind that harmonize our inner and outer lives. They bring
peace to ourselves and freedom from fear to those with whom we share
our world, as we saw in chapter 6.

An important—and comforting—fact is that the words *good* and *bad*
are not traditionally used in Buddhist discussions of morality. Rather,
intentional actions (karma), whether bodily, verbal, or mental, are considered *skillful* if they cause no harm to ourselves or others and *unskillful*
if they do result in any form of suffering. A great blessing of developing
the sacred perfection of ethical integrity is that we gain freedom from
the guilt and remorse that may have been built into our consciousness.

Many of us raised in families or religions where guilt and remorse were
used as weapons to control our behavior may react in three stages to this
notion: First, eliminating notions of good and bad may initially elicit a
warm sense of relief. Second, this relief diminishes when we realize that
it is *we* who must judge, control, and be responsible for our own acts. It's
an inside job, in many ways more challenging than reporting to some outside authority or code. Third, we realize one of the great teaching gifts

of the Buddha: we can intentionally learn heart characteristics such as ethical integrity if we are willing to make the commitment and cultivate the mindfulness to doing so.

Dhammapala suggests that we reflect on the perfection of virtue with these thoughts:

> Even the water of the Ganges cannot wash away the stain of hatred, but yet the water of virtue is able to do so. Even yellow sandalwood cannot cool the fever of lust, yet virtue is able to remove it. Virtue is the unique adornment of the good, surpassing the adornments cherished by ordinary people, such as necklaces, diadems, and earrings. It is a sweet-smelling fragrance superior to incense as it pervades all directions and is always in place.

It is "sweet-smelling" and "always in place"—if it has been cultivated and is perfected in two aspects: avoidance of unskillful actions and performance of skillful actions, a pairing that links it to such other ideals as renunciation, loving-kindness, and equanimity.

Cultivating Ethical Integrity

Ethical integrity follows generosity because it purifies both the giver and the receiver and leads to dispelling unskillful behavior: it is the opposite of greed, hatred, and delusion. The perfection of ethical integrity is twofold: First, the cultivation of it transforms our *external* actions— our behavior; our speech, action, and livelihood—from harmful to wise, which purifies old "bad" karma into future "good" karma. Second, the practice of ethical integrity purifies our *interior* virtues—our understanding, intention, effort, mindfulness, and concentration—which transforms our heart-mind. This internal transformation then produces skillful speech and actions. In this way ethical integrity creates accord between our inner and outer life.

What this means for us is that if we have the faith and mindfulness to pursue a spiritual path, the most immediate manifestations can be in our actions and words, even as we cultivate the corresponding inner qualities. Does this mean that we can judge people by their actions? Maybe. If their actions are unskillful and harm themselves and others, the unskillfulness is usually apparent, though guessing at their intentions is a dangerous presumption. More useful is trying to discern if *our* intentions are skillful or not, by reflecting honestly upon our own words and actions.

This kind of reflection is an important component of living our lives as spiritual practice. In an important lesson to his son, Rahula, the Buddha asked Rahula what a mirror is for. "For reflection," Rahula answered. The Buddha then said, "In the same way, bodily actions, verbal actions, and mental actions are to be done with repeated reflection." Before we take action, we must reflect *ahead of time* as to whether it will be unskillful and cause suffering to ourselves or others. *During the action and afterward*, we should reflect similarly. We should use all three times as opportunities to refrain from unskillful actions and should do only those actions that have positive consequences for oneself and others. Those who purify all their actions only do so through repeated reflections in this way.

We seem to have built-in "virtue detectors" that are activated when we reflect on our own actions. When we have acted skillfully, we do not experience the dissatisfaction that arises when we have in some way caused ourselves or others suffering. If we feel uncomfortable, we should ask ourselves, "What's going on here?" Discomfort and other aversive feelings such as shame are sure signs that we have acted in a way that we need to examine. We can't really undo past acts, though making amends or apologizing can help us in our commitment not to do the same thing again—that is, not to reenact old "bad" karma. Chapter 8 gives us some specific techniques for avoiding this hazard.

Cultivating the Five Precepts

Chapter 6 mentioned how laypeople could give the gift of fearlessness— one of the three most important manifestations of generosity—by living according to the training guidelines known as the five precepts.

When we take the precepts, we commit ourselves to the training to abstain (1) from harming living beings, (2) from taking what is not given freely, (3) from sexual misconduct, (4) from false speech, and (5) from the abuse of intoxicating substances. Most religions and ethical philosophies have lists of "dos and don'ts" that are remarkably similar. The five precepts differ from these other codes in one very important way: they are not commandments according to which some other authority will judge us but rather are reflections of the way spiritually evolved beings act. The burden is on us—if we want to pursue the path of spiritual beings, we act the way they act, to the best of our ability.

We shall look more closely below at each of the five precepts. As well as looking at the "avoidance" aspects of each precept, we'll also look at the "performance" of their positive opposites, since both sides are important to mindfully cultivating virtue. For example, in additional to avoiding harming living beings, we must also actively try to benefit living beings. We'll begin our discussion of each with the Buddha's observations about each precept, from Bhikkhu Bodhi's translation of Anguttara Nikaya 8:39.

1. To abstain from harming living beings

> Here, a noble disciple, having abandoned the destruction of life, abstains from the destruction of life. By abstaining from the destruction of life, the noble disciple gives to an immeasurable number of beings freedom from fear, enmity, and affliction. He himself in turn enjoys immeasurable freedom from fear, enmity, and affliction. This is the first gift, a great gift, primal, of long standing, traditional, ancient, unadulterated and never before adulterated, which is not being adulterated and will not be adulterated, not repudiated by wise ascetics and brahmins.

What a different world we would live in if all people embraced this precept. What a blessing of freedom it would be for women to be able to enjoy a walk alone on a starlit night without fear, for children of any ethnic group to go into a new neighborhood to play without fear, for battered adults to await their spouses without fear, for people of the Middle East to greet arriving Americans with joy and not fear. When I visited Costa Rica a number of years ago, I got a sense of what could happen if even a small country decided to get rid of its standing army and put the money into health care, education, and the environment: everyone wins.

When we abstain from harming other beings, we not only give them freedom from fear, we also give ourselves freedom from fear (and shame and remorse) because of the karmic results of our actions. As we noted in chapter 3, we have the opportunity to plant "seeds" of either suffering or happiness, but whichever we choose *will* bear fruit when the conditions are right. Our karma can be individual or family or even national or species; as an individual we swat an insect, as a family we ignore and thus perpetuate physical or emotional child abuse, as a nation we exploit the resources of other cultures, or as a species we contribute to atmospheric pollution and global warming. The implications are far-reaching, To repeat: not harming others is truly a win-win situation for individuals, families, nations, even species.

As we cultivate abstaining from harming others, we can also find positive expressions of this precept. Instead of interacting with others with harm, animosity, and oppression, we can make a commitment to ourselves to mindfully relate with compassion, kindness, and help.

Once, when I made a major change in my life and livelihood, I decided that I should do a formal strategic plan, complete with mission statement, goals, and financial expectations, all against a timeline with checkpoints. As so many corporate planners have discovered, the greatest challenge in such an undertaking is the mission statement, an accurate expression of mission/vision/goal in a few words. The longer I tried to create a mission statement about what I wanted to *do* and what I wanted to *get*, the more frustrated I became. I finally realized that I was making this life change because of who I wanted to *be*, and then I easily wrote a mission statement that I have lived comfortably with for more than a decade. Instead of net profit, the currency became mindfulness, compassion, kindness. Instead of seeing what I could squeeze out of the world, I envisioned what I did not want to add: another drop of harm or pain. I did not want to fray my interconnectedness with all of life.

2. To abstain from taking what is not given freely

> Again, a noble disciple, having abandoned the taking of what is not given, abstains from taking what is not given. By abstaining from taking what is not given, the noble disciple gives to an immeasurable number of beings freedom from fear, enmity, and affliction. He himself in turn enjoys immeasurable freedom from fear, enmity, and affliction. This is the second gift...

This precept is about so much more than stealing. It also involves *any* kind of dishonesty, misappropriation, or exploitation—all of which are the opposite of generosity and express greed, the origin of suffering. Any time we take what is not freely given, we are karmically stoking the fires of future suffering.

Some kinds of stealing are easy to identify—shoplifting, cheating on taxes or expense accounts, claiming as our own some object that isn't. But if we are mindful about cultivating this precept, we will view many new areas of our life from the perspective of stealing—such as environmental concerns, clothing, parenting, working. We've never asked ourselves what our fair share truly is.

When we look at environmental misappropriation as a nation, we must face the fact that the United States consists of less than 5 percent of the world's population but uses almost 25 percent of the world's natural resources. When we look at power use for transportation, appliances, heating and cooling, for example, we can easily see ways we just "take": driving low-mileage vehicles instead of walking, bicycling, car-pooling, or taking public transportation; driving at excessive speeds that lower fuel efficiency; leaving lights and appliances on when they are not in use; using watt-guzzling lightbulbs; setting thermostats excessively high or low and not sealing windows, doors, and roofs in ways that would lessen heat transfer.

Another thing we take is power—by exploiting people. This may happen as close to home as "bullying" our children or parents. It can happen in the workplace in the way we treat coworkers or those who work for us. It can happen almost anywhere in the world when we exercise excessive privilege because of our age, gender, nationality, race, etc. The clothing and objects that come to us from sweatshops fall into this category.

Because all of life is interconnected, when we take what is not freely given, we steal from ourselves. In the same vein, when we give something freely—sometimes even when it has not been asked for—we are being generous to ourselves. To work with this precept in a positive way, we can reinforce the generous acts we considered in chapter 6, and we can mindfully consider not merely what we take but also what we use and what we buy.

3. To abstain from sexual misconduct

> Again, a noble disciple, having abandoned sexual misconduct, abstains from sexual misconduct. By abstaining from sexual misconduct, the noble disciple gives to an immeasurable number of beings freedom from fear, enmity, and affliction. He himself in turn enjoys immeasurable freedom from fear, enmity, and affliction. This is the third gift...

Freedom from danger, freedom from animosity, and freedom from oppression—these are the gifts that we give to others and to ourselves by keeping this precept. The Buddha enumerated various categories of people with whom we should avoid sexual intimacy, including anyone who is in a committed relationship or who is not our partner in our committed relationship. Also on the "no" list is any sexual act where physical or emotional force is used. Put simply, this precept stresses refraining from harming anyone through sexual acts. Period.

In addition to abstaining from harming through sex, we can cultivate the positive side of sexual intimacy by reflecting on ways we can develop a committed relationship that is typified by loving-kindness and compassion rather than lust—a relationship where sexual intimacy is but one expression of the nonselfish love between people.

4. To abstain from false speech

> Again, a noble disciple, having abandoned false speech, abstains from false speech. By abstaining from false speech, the noble disciple gives to an immeasurable number of beings freedom from fear, enmity, and affliction. He himself in turn enjoys immeasurable freedom from fear, enmity, and affliction. This is the fourth gift...

When I first began to read books about Buddhism, I was quite struck that in every major teaching collection, the topic of speech got its own section, rather than being included within the category of wise action; that speech got its own precept; and that speech got its own listing separate from morality among the perfections. Such is the power of speech, as anyone who has seriously tried to cultivate wise speech has learned. The Buddha stressed in many teachings that we must never indulge in falsehoods, but lies are just one kind of unwise speech. He also urged us to avoid speech that would be difficult to hear because it was uttered in anger or in some other way that created aversion. We'll look at all these other aspects in chapter 12, "Truthfulness."

5. To abstain from the use of intoxicating substances

> Again, a noble disciple, having abandoned liquor, wine, and intoxicants, the basis for heedlessness, abstains from liquor, wine, and intoxicants, the basis for heedlessness. By abstaining from liquor, wine, and intoxicants, the basis for heedless-

ness, the noble disciple gives to an immeasurable number of beings freedom from fear, enmity, and affliction. He himself in turn enjoys immeasurable freedom from fear, enmity, and affliction. This is the fifth gift...

Considering the fact that there are only five precepts for laypeople, it's remarkable that one—20 percent of the total—is about abusing intoxicants, that such a relatively simple thing would have the same great rewards as the others. I believe that there are two major reasons for the weight given to this precept.

First, the goal of spiritual practice is enlightenment, which is based on maintaining mindfulness, seeing the world clearly, and acting in ways that harm no beings—all actions that are distorted by intoxicants. The precepts tell us how enlightened beings act, and no beings seeking enlightenment would intentionally ingest a substance that would negate these aspects of their path.

Second, people who abuse intoxicants are more likely to violate one or more of the other four precepts. For example, hundreds of thousands of beings have been killed or maimed in automobile accidents involving intoxication. Prisons are jammed with inmates who have committed violent acts while intoxicated, including homicide, battery, and rape. Intoxication often precipitates abusive and harmful speech and is a common factor in sexual liaisons that cause remorse and harm to self or others.

All of the precepts express nonharming and give the gift of freedom from fear. When we live in accordance with the precepts, we create a safe and sacred space for all with whom we share our world.

The Ten Precepts of a Zen Peacemaker

Different schools of Buddhism observe different numbers of precepts—Vipassana, my tradition, follows the five enumerated above. The Zen Peacemaker Order, founded by Roshi Bernie Glassman as a way to link social activism and Zen Buddhism and to realize and activate the interconnectedness of life, articulates ten. For those of us who wish to actively live our spiritual practice within the context of society's challenges, it can be very useful to reflect on these practices:

Being Mindful of the interdependence of Oneness and Diversity, and wishing to actualize my vows, I engage in the spiritual practices of:

1. Recognizing that I am not separate from all that is.
   This is the precept of Non-Killing.
2. Being satisfied with what I have.
   This is the precept of Non-Stealing.
3. Encountering all creations with respect and dignity.
   This is the precept of Chaste Conduct.
4. Listening and speaking from the heart.
   This is the precept of Non-Lying.
5. Cultivating a mind that sees clearly.
   This is the precept of Not Being Ignorant.
6. Unconditionally accepting what each moment has to offer.
   This is the precept of Not Talking about Others' Errors and Faults.
7. Speaking what I perceive to be the truth without guilt or blame.
   This is the precept of Not Elevating Oneself and Blaming Others.
8. Using all of the ingredients of my life.
   This is the precept of Not Being Stingy.
9. Transforming suffering into wisdom.
   This is the precept of Not Being Angry.
10. Honoring my life as an instrument of peacemaking.
    This is the precept of Not Thinking Ill of the Three Treasures [the Buddha, the Dharma, and the Sangha].

Practice and Reflection: Ethical Integrity

1. Can intentional actions be viewed as skillful or unskillful depending on their outcomes, or do you believe that some actions are inherently good or evil? Why?

2. Reflect on the five precepts. Are there other precepts that you would add to this list for householders? Would you add any of the ten precepts used by the Zen Peacemakers?

3. How strictly do you observe the precept to abstain from harming living beings?

   • Do you kill insects in your home? In your workplace? In public places such as restaurants?

   • Are you a vegetarian? Why or why not?

   • Do you engage in self-destructive behavior such as abusing food?

   • Would you euthanize a pet who is in extreme pain?

   • Should terminally ill people in extreme pain have the right to suicide?

4. How strictly do you observe the precept to abstain from taking what is not freely given?

   • Do you ever distort your taxes or expense reports?

   • Do you ever break into a long line at a concert, movie, or other public gathering?

   • Are you cautious in your use of water, such as not taking long showers or leaving the water running while you brush your teeth or shave?

- When buying a car, how important is mileage to you?

- Do you consider where and how things you buy were made?

- Do you boycott any companies or countries because of their human rights or environmental policies?

- Is excessive packaging a consideration in your purchasing?

5. How strictly do you observe the precept to abstain from sexual misconduct?

- Would dressing in a provocative manner be considered sexual misconduct?

- Is casual flirting sexual misconduct?

- If both partners agree to an open relationship, is it skillful for one or both to be sexually intimate with others?

- Have you ever felt remorse because of sexual thoughts or actions?

6. How strictly do you observe the precept to abstain from false speech?

- Do you exaggerate events in retelling a story to make it more spellbinding?

- When you retell a story, do you minimize your involvement in the events to make your role less impactful?

7. How strictly do you observe the precept to abstain from abusing intoxicating substances?

- Does a glass of wine or a beer with dinner count as an intoxicating substance?

- Do you ever use a substance to dull emotional pain? Is this abuse?

- Do you ever use a substance to dull physical pain? Is this abuse?

- Do you ever put others at risk by your use of intoxicating substances?

- Have you ever been abusive verbally or physically after using intoxicating substances?

- Do you believe that people who harm others by breaking this precept are unskillful or are bad people?

8. Do you have the faith to resolve to cultivate the sacred ideal of ethical integrity in your life?

9. Sit quietly for ten minutes and do a meditation practice using the repetition of these phrases as the object of your concentration/mindfulness. As you silently repeat the phrases, do so slowly enough to feel what each one would be like in your life:

> May I be happy.
> May I be healthy.
> May I live in safety.
> May I give freedom from fear to all beings.

8.
Renunciation

Resolution: May I renounce and let go of anything that does not lead to liberation and compassion for all beings.

Mantra: May I let go of ever harming other beings.

A FAMILIAR ADAGE CLAIMS "You can't think your way into right acting, but you can act your way into right thinking." For me, this maxim describes refining the ideal of renunciation through perfecting its fundamental achievement: letting go. In normal everyday life, it's unlikely that anyone, particularly someone new to a spiritual path, in the face of temptation would spontaneously have the thought: "Renunciation would be a good idea now." But over time, as we intentionally develop the spiritual perfections of the heart-mind, seriously considering letting go—or sometimes just letting be—becomes almost reflexive.

The Power of Sense Pleasures

In his provocative essay "Trading Candy for Gold," contemporary monk-scholar Thanissaro Bhikkhu observes that the widely recognized American pursuit of happiness causes us conflict when we face the choice of a lesser happiness in exchange for a greater one—analogous to trading a bag of candy for a pound of gold. We want both.

In this case, the "candy" is anything our senses crave and the "gold" is virtue. Appetite for sense pleasures is the very craving that is the source of suffering, because its objects are always impermanent—candy never lasts. Really, we should give up our bag of candy for the bag of gold. But throughout history, the challenge of delaying gratification for a greater good has, for many, marked the most difficult aspect of spiritual growth.

When we're caught in the throes of desire for sense pleasure, it's hard to appreciate the value of virtue. Until one can see and believe that the avoidance of unskillful actions (for instance, eating a whole bag of candy) is the foundation for our spiritual growth, the gold will be perceived as fool's gold.

The perfection of ethical integrity as described in the preceding chapter is both *developed* through renunciation and also *manifests* as further renunciation.

Ethical integrity involves the purification of external behavior and freeing oneself from the chains of sense pleasures; renunciation is the purification of interior behavior. Renunciation makes it possible to fulfill the perfection of ethical integrity through understanding the unsatisfactoriness of sense pleasures. Deep comprehension of the inadequacy of sense pleasures is absolutely critical to cultivating renunciation. Dhammapala sums up renunciation and gives striking similes for sense pleasures:

> The perfection of renunciation is the wholesome act of consciousness which occurs renouncing sense pleasures... preceded by the perception of their unsatisfactoriness and accompanied by compassion and skillful means... Sense pleasures, like a drop of honey smeared over the blade of a sword, give limited satisfaction and entail abundant harm. They are fleeting like a show perceived in a flash of lightning; enjoyable only through a perversion of perception like the adornments of a madman; a means of vengeance like a camouflaged pit of excrement; unsatisfying like a thin drink or the water moistening the fingers; afflictive like food which is inwardly rotten; a cause for calamity like a baited hook;... inwardly burning like the fire in the hollow of a tree;... and giving little satisfaction like a chain of bones.

The way to give more value to the gold than to the candy is to reflect on our sense pleasures and passions with wisdom; understand the nature of suffering, impermanence, karma, and not-self; and make a commitment to nonharming. As our actions become more skillful, we will increasingly experience first relief, then blissful freedom from the imprisoning "chain of bones."

An important insight into what happens when we abandon restraint and let the sense pleasures rule is related in Samyutta Nikaya 35. In this parable, a man ties six animals together with strong rope, then sets chase to them. Each of the six animals would pull toward its own natural habitat until it was exhausted. Then the animals would give up and would come under the influence of the strongest among them. This depicts lack of restraint among the senses.

Then the Buddha twists this parable to show what happens when there is restraint: In the same way, when a person whose mindfulness immersed in the body is undeveloped, all the senses pull toward their natural source of pleasure. When there is restraint, the person catches the six animals and binds them with a strong rope, which he then tethers to a strong post. Then those six animals would each pull toward its own habitat until all six were exhausted and would stand, sit, or lie down right there next to the post.

In the same way, when a person whose mindfulness immersed in the body is developed and pursued, the senses do not pull toward their various objects. This is restraint. The strong post is a phrase used for mindfulness immersed in the body. When all our senses are pulling in opposite directions, we may be disturbed enough to want to calm and restrain them. But sometimes we feel as if we're swept up in a floodtide of pleasant sensations, and it's even more difficult to foresee the whirlpools and waterfalls that lie ahead. In these situations, we can use mindfulness to tie ourselves to a post, to resist being swept away by desire.

A "Self" Through Sense Pleasures and Pain

We know the world through our senses.

In this knowing, there are three primary phenomena that affect our present and future ease and dis-ease. First, with conscious sense contact, we usually experience the object of that sense as either pleasant or unpleasant (if it's neutral, we may not even be aware of the contact). Second, depending upon the feeling of pleasant or unpleasant, we experience desire or aversion causing us to "grasp" or "push away" the object of the sense. Finally, the combination of perception through the senses and concurrent feelings create a sense of self. Instead of saying, "*The eye* sees the sunset," we say, "*I* see the sunset." Instead of saying, "*The mind* fantasizes about a sexual encounter," we say, "*I* am fantasizing about a sexual encounter."

As long as we identify the sense experience as our self, it is very difficult to renounce sense pleasures.

When we contemplate impermanence and not-self, we are inclined to let go of sense pleasures as *the* source of happiness. We can see that the immediate gratification of a sense desire that violates our principles of morality is better relinquished. The gold begins to be of greater value than the candy.

Discern What to Renounce

Mindfulness, especially mindfulness meditation, is a critical component in cultivating renunciation. If you are not aware that you are experiencing tugs or even passions through the sense gates, you obviously will not abandon them; a foundation for discerning such tugs is laid each time we do mindfulness meditation and become skilled in recognizing the arising of the five hindrances.

Another underpinning of renunciation is insightful observance of the five precepts; discerning that there is a sense contact to restrain and insight to be recognized is a critical component of wisdom. Both on the cushion and off, we use mindfulness to observe the objects of our senses with bare awareness so that we do not embellish our sense experiences with flights of fantasy and elaborate stories. For it is when we separate the sense from its object that we can, first, not identify our self as the sense and, second, renounce the object of the sense if it leads us into unskillful behavior. Of all the sense gates, the one with the most impact on our behavior is the mind. As Upasika Kee Nanayon, the foremost twentieth-century woman teacher in Thailand, noted in her book *Stop, Look, and Let Go*: "We have to focus on the mind, which is the factor in charge, the stem point. If we exercise restraint over the mind, then that, in and of itself, keeps all the sense doors restrained. The mind has nothing but attachments and feelings of self, giving rise to all sorts of suffering simply from its lack of restraint. This is something we've all experienced."

In his teachings the Buddha related discernment and renunciation to the Four Noble Truths and the end of suffering: he stressed that when we can discern suffering, its nature and cause, we can discern direct knowledge of its purpose so that we can abandon it.

Mindfulness of the Sense Gates through Eating

As we begin turning our everyday life into spiritual practice, we start by focusing on things we do every day, such as breathing and eating. These activities are where our true teachers are and where our commitment must be. Our relationship to food may not seem to obstruct liberation and compassion for all as much as, say, the Berlin Wall or solitary confinement in prison, but it certainly can be such an impediment in our personal lives.

I use eating as a focus for everyday practice in two chapters of this book: here and chapter 4. I sometimes think my entire practice could be around food, so well does it lend itself to awakening mindfulness through all the senses. A beginning exploration of renunciation is very effectively centered around food, which so often stimulates all our senses. Consider how some examples of sense qualities play out around food:

Eye Gate

I never saw a donut I didn't want.

When I pass by a donut display case, I immediately spot the different varieties. My eye is drawn to the hole in the side of the jelly donuts, and I know, by sight alone, whether they're filled with raspberry or strawberry jelly. There is an instantaneous connection between my eyes and my mouth, which fills with saliva.

There's nothing inherently wrong with liking donuts, though some health considerations, such as diabetes, may limit intake. The point is to observe what happens when the eye sense gate triggers greed ("I want them all"), grasping ("I'll just buy three"), and delusion ("This time will be different, and they won't upset my stomach").

We can also experience aversion through sight alone—as can be attested by the generations of youngsters who gagged at the sight of broccoli or by those who lose their appetite when everything on a plate is the same color.

We can learn much about the wanting mind that causes suffering through our visual sense gate. Eye sense is not self. Can you restrain the eye gate?

Smell Gate

From candy stores on the Atlantic City Boardwalk to bakeries in San Francisco's North Beach, vendors have learned the lessons of "piping" the scents of their wares—sometimes enhanced—to the sidewalks so that passersby are seduced into their stores. Similarly, many supermarkets sell scented candles with names like "Pumpkin Friend" and "Cinnamon Buns" so that people having others over for brunch or Thanksgiving dinner can whet their guests' appetites through association.

On the other hand, when you return from a vacation and discover milk or leftovers or some delicacy left in the refrigerator, you may need to hold your breath to avoid the smell while you throw these odiferous leftovers away. Often I find that such stinks will kill my appetite for several hours afterward.

One thing we can sometimes learn through our sense of smell is the presence of expectations: for example, I have never drunk coffee that tasted as good as it smelled while the beans were being ground. Coffee that might otherwise taste perfectly delicious seems disappointing due to the expectations set by my own smell gate.

Sense of smell is not self. Can you restrain your smell gate?

Ear Gate

When we were young, many of us heard the frequent chant "Close your mouth when you chew." Something about the sound of chomping or slurping has raised great aversion in American parents for decades. But there is nothing innately "bad" about making sounds when we eat; in some cultures doing so is considered good manners, a way of showing appreciation for the good taste.

Some cooks capitalize on the appealing sounds of cooking food; Chinese restaurants offer such specialties as "Sizzling Go Ba," "Sizzling Lobster and Beef," even "Sizzling Rice Soup." Some establishments bring the sizzle right to your table by preparing your dinner in front of you to enhance your enjoyment of the food.

And if you eat too much, sound has been used in an advertising campaign for reprieve: "Plop, plop. Fizz, fizz. Oh, what a relief it is."

Hearing is not self. Can you restrain your ear gate?

Touch Gate

Sometimes, and to some people, the quality of the texture of a food can determine whether it's desirable or not. Some people eat only crispy raw vegetables, while others cook vegetables into mush. These desired textures can have much to do with cultural, ethnic, or regional background—and memory. I've met very few people not born in the southern United States who like boiled okra ("It's slimy") or grits ("I'd as soon eat sawdust"). Many people who like steamed lobster want nothing to do with "that gooey green stuff" inside; others love it. Eating raw fish ("Rubbery") is an acquired custom in many cultures, and some people who tried a raw oyster once will never eat another one ("It felt like I was eating phlegm"). Paying attention to our reactions to food's textures and temperatures can give us interesting clues as to the role of touch in many other areas of our lives, from the temperature of a shower to the weave of a bedsheet.

Touch is not self. Can you restrain your touch gate?

Taste Gate

Most of us have highly refined "taste buds" and know almost as soon as we put something in our mouth whether the taste is pleasant or unpleasant.

In some cases, the pleasantness precipitates a state of near addiction. This well-understood theme has been picked up in numerous advertising campaigns with lines such as "Bet you can't eat just one." We see these conditioned preferences when people add salt, for example, to food before they taste it.

What we often consider "taste" may well be a complex of several senses: taste, smell, touch, sight, even sound. When we have a head cold and our noses are stopped up, our sense of taste may be diminished almost completely; we may not feel particularly hungry until we are assailed by the odor of baking pizza and find ourselves salivating; we may lose our appetite quickly if food is too mushy or the wrong temperature—think cold, watery oatmeal; seeing a bowl of truffles on a table may cause us the irresistible urge to reach for one, or two, or more; and remember all those sizzling foods and fizzy drinks.

Taste is not self. Can you restrain your taste gate?

Mind Gate

The power of any of the previous senses can pale in comparison to the mind sense.

We get to watch our mind sense every time someone asks, "What would you like for dinner?" or we study the menu of a good restaurant where we have not previously eaten. In the latter case, we may evaluate unusual dishes such as prawns with mango salsa even if we have never tasted them; we imagine what they taste like and decide whether we want to order them or not. As Upasika Kee Nanayon stressed, when we can cultivate mental restraint, we simultaneously cultivate restraint over all the senses. We learn to think or say, "I've had enough," or "No" (which is a complete sentence). Mind is not self. Can you restrain your mind gate?

The importance of guarding and restraining our sense gates was related in one of the Buddha's memorable Jataka Tales: One evening a hard-shell tortoise was foraging for food along the shoreline of a lake. Nearby a jackal was also wandering around searching for his evening meal. The tortoise saw the jackal first, so—withdrawing its four legs, with its neck as a fifth limb, into its own shell—the tortoise remained perfectly still. But the jackal had already spotted the tortoise from afar; it ran over and hovered around ready to pounce on it and eat it as soon as the tortoise stretched out its legs or its neck. But the tortoise didn't stretch out from its shell. The jackal, after a long wait and not having gotten any opportunity to catch part of the tortoise, lost interest and left. The Buddha noted through this story that Mara is continuously hovering around us, hoping for the opportunity to snatch one of our sense gates—especially the mind—so we should always have the doors to our senses well-defended.

Practice and Reflection: The Senses

1. Reflect on the fact that a sense is a sense, not a self.

- Look at one hand. Reflect on the fact that the eye, not the self, sees the hand.

- Clap the hands together. Reflect that the sense of touch, not the self, feels the skin. Reflect that the ear, not the self, hears the sound.

- Looking at one hand, imagine it as old and wrinkled—or young and smooth. Reflect that the mind, not the self, perceives the process of aging.

2. Is it easy or difficult for you to exchange a lesser, immediate happiness for a greater, long-term happiness—to exchange candy for gold?

  - Is your virtue conditional on circumstances? For example, if you could have an illicit affair with the sexual partner of your dreams without anyone discovering this affair, would you? Honestly? Why or why not?

  - Do you ever take excessively long showers because they feel good even though you're wasting water?

  - Do you ever drive faster than the highway speed limit even though you know you're getting lower fuel mileage? If yes, why?

  - Do you keep your thermostat low and wear sweaters indoors during the winter to conserve power?

  - Have you made any lifestyle changes to conserve natural resources?

  - If you wanted to lose ten pounds before you put on a bathing suit next summer, would you use a "crash" diet, or would you change your exercise and nutrition program permanently?

  - If you change your diet and exercise patterns to lose weight, do you stop that "program" when you have met your goal?

3. Which of your senses is dominant? Does this information help you to cultivate renunciation?

- Are you more susceptible to radio or to TV food advertising? Neither? Both?

- When you walk through a supermarket, do you impulsively buy items not on your grocery list? In the fresh-vegetable department? In the ice cream freezer?

- Do any smells elicit childhood memories—such as tangerines and Christmas or chicken soup and illness?

- Does the sound of burping elicit an aversive response from you? If the burper is your dinner partner? If the burper is a baby? If the burper is a dog?

- Do you enjoy a cup of lukewarm coffee or tea? Is the taste different from that of a hot beverage, or is sense of touch the main factor in your enjoyment?

- Gather several food items with different tastes: salty (peanut, potato chip); artificially sweetened (candy, any dessert); and sour (lemon or other citrus). One at a time, put each taste item into your mouth and hold it there for about a minute. Where on your tongue do you perceive each taste? Which taste is strongest? Which taste do you prefer? Did you have a strong desire to have more of any of an item?

4. Do you restrain your impulse to eat or overeat particular foods on the basis of "willpower" alone or after some thought-through understanding of consequences such as weight gain or allergy or indigestion? Do you eat any particular foods that you do not find especially pleasant because of consequences?

5. When you are hungry, prepare a plate or bowl of your very favorite food and spend ten minutes reflecting on your sense responses to its presence—but do not eat it until instructed to do so.

- Which sense gate is most affected—eyes, nose, mind?

- Does seeing or smelling the food bring up any associations for you? Do you remember where you first ate it?

- How strong is your desire for this food? How is that desire manifesting—for example, through salivation or thoughts about how much you want it?

- Take one bite, then wait for a minute and reflect on what senses are affected and whether the food tastes as good as you thought it would. Take another bite, wait, and reflect; then another and another until the food is gone. Notice if the time between bites shrinks.

- Did the last bite taste as good as the first? Did you crave more? Why did you restrain this urge—or did you give in to it? Why?

6. Do you have the resolve to let go of anything that obstructs liberation and compassion for all beings, including yourself?

7. Sit quietly for ten minutes and do a meditation practice using the repetition of these phrases as the object of your

concentration/mindfulness. As you silently repeat the phrases, do so slowly enough to feel what each one would be like in your life:

> May I be happy.
> May I be healthy.
> May I live in safety.
> May I let go of ever harming other beings.

9.
Wisdom

Resolution: With discernment and insight, may I make
choices that lead to compassion and liberation.

Mantra: May my choices be wise and compassionate.

Translating *Wisdom*

THE LANGUAGE IN WHICH the Buddha's teachings were first recorded is the ancient Pali language. The word in Pali, Sanskrit, and some more modern Asian languages for "mind" is *citta,* which means both "heart" and "mind." Thus, to begin to understand wisdom, we must do so within the context of heart-mind: the compassionate mind of awakening.

Language and translation present other challenges in exploring the perfection of wisdom. Some Pali words simply do not have adequate English equivalents—sometimes because of the concepts involved (for example, citta and dukkha), sometimes because of the connotations with which a word has become encrusted over time. In Pali, the word *panna* (in Sanskrit, *prajna*) for centuries was traditionally translated as "wisdom," but the connotations of that word have varied with time, culture, language, and, in Buddhism, tradition. The contemporary scholar-monk Bhikkhu Bodhi, in his English translation of Dhammapala's *Treatise on the Paramis* from the Pali, uses the word "wisdom." Another contemporary scholar-monk, Thanissaro Bhikkhu, in his translations of the Pali Canon, uses the word "discernment" for *panna.*

When we read their texts closely, we find that there really isn't a contradiction in their differing usage and that it is instructive to see how these translations mesh. In one passage of the *Treatise*, for example, we read that "Wisdom has the characteristic of penetrating the real specific nature (of phenomena)," which certainly is inclusive of the definition of the word "discernment"—to see something that is not very clear, or to differentiate.

What Is Wisdom?

As I mused on the linguistic challenges of *panna,* I found myself staring at a Tibetan painting of Manjushri, the embodiment of wisdom. His traditional depiction shows him holding in one hand a flaming sword that he wields to slash through ignorance and delusion; in the other hand, he holds a scripture supported by a lotus. As is frequently the case where this Buddhist image is displayed, on my wall next to it is a companion painting of Avalokiteshvara, the embodiment of compassion, since wisdom and compassion are seen as the two characteristics necessary for acting skillfully. They are united in the concept of heart-mind and are sometimes described as the two wings of awakening.

The intention and ability to act skillfully for the benefit of others have been accepted attributes of Western concepts of wisdom since ancient times: Aristotle defined wisdom as knowledge of causes; Cicero said its function is to discriminate between good and evil. So the relationship between wisdom and virtue has been long and widely accepted. Sometimes "virtue" is viewed as following a set of proscriptions and prescriptions; sometimes it is seen as simply common sense. Even Mark Twain had an opinion: "The perfection of wisdom... is to proportion our wants to our possessions, our ambitions to our capacities, we will then be a happy and a virtuous people."

When we come to comprehend the Four Noble Truths, we come to see that ultimate wisdom is the pursuit of enduring happiness—not fleeting happiness—for oneself and all other beings. And the Buddha told us that wisdom, like all the perfections, is a heart characteristic that we can learn.

Cultivating Wisdom

When Dhammapala considered wisdom within the sequence of perfections, he noted:

> Wisdom is mentioned immediately after renunciation: (a) because renunciation is perfected and purified by wisdom; (b) to show that there is no wisdom in the absence of meditation, since concentration is the proximate cause of wisdom and wisdom the manifestation of concentration; (c) in order to list the causal basis for equanimity immediately after the causal basis for serenity; and (d) to show that skillful means in working for the welfare of others springs from meditation directed to their welfare.

The point about concentration being wisdom's proximate cause is noteworthy here. The Buddha stated repeatedly that we gain insight into the reality of phenomena through direct experience. We are able to do so when we have cultivated concentration; it is within deep meditative absorption that we learn through direct experience about impermanence, karma, and not-self. Yes, we must acquire knowledge, understanding, of wisdom. This understanding is the motivation for cultivating the other perfections. At the same time, concentration is the vehicle for true wisdom, which leads in turn to living for the benefit of all beings. Concentration will ensure our own well-being and equanimity, so that we may live skillfully.

According to Dhammapala, in order to perfect wisdom, we must understand the Four Noble Truths, and we must accompany that understanding with compassion and skillful means. In addition to merely comprehending the Four Noble Truths, the Buddha said that we have four tasks, one for each truth:

1. **Dukkha**: *Our task is to understand it.* We must grasp that dukkha includes birth, aging, illness, death, being with what is unpleasant, being separated from what is pleasant.
2. **Origin of dukkha**: *Our task is to eliminate it.* Eradicating the source of dukkha involves understanding its origination—clinging to the five collectives (material form, feeling, perception, mental formations, and consciousness) and seeing them as permanent and part of our "self." Generosity and renunciation are important in the task of overcoming the origin of dukkha.
3. **Cessation of dukkha**: *Our task is to make it happen.* With understanding of the nature of dukkha and its origin, we are moved to end it. Energy, patience, and determination are helpful.
4. **Path to the end of dukkha**: *Our task is to follow the Noble Eightfold Path.* We must cultivate wise understanding, wise intention, wise speech, wise action, wise livelihood, wise effort, wise mindfulness, and wise concentration. All of the perfections come into play as we follow this path.

We cultivate wisdom by fulfilling these tasks.

The Wisdom of Emptiness

So far we have considered wisdom primarily from the perspective of Theravada Buddhism—the branch of Buddhism predominant in Southeast Asia. But our exploration would be incomplete without at least touching briefly on the teachings of Mahayana Buddhism, which is the branch most popular in China, Japan, Korea, northern Asia, and Tibet.

Mahayana Buddhism presents us with the idea of *prajnaparamita*, the perfection of wisdom. The major source for these teachings are the *Prajnaparamita Sutras*, a collection of about forty sutras, many from Tibet and China, in texts written in Sanskrit and Chinese that may date back to as early as 179 CE. This collection stresses that wisdom must be directly experienced and intuitive, not conceptual; that all phenomena are empty of self; and that some equate full realization of emptiness with enlightenment.

The most well known of the prajnaparamita teachings are the Diamond Sutra and the Heart Sutra. It is not possible to summarize either of these compelling sutras in a few words; there are tens of thousands of commentaries in many languages for both. I personally have found those in English by Thich Nhat Hanh to be especially accessible and "user-friendly" for Westerners.

The Diamond Sutra highlights the great vow of buddhas-to-be to lead all beings to liberation. This vow inspires us to ask ourselves, as Thich Nhat Hanh does in *The Diamond That Cuts Through Illusion*, his commentaries to this sutra: "Is this vow at all related to my life and the life of my community? Are we practicing for ourselves or for others?" Here, too, wisdom and compassion are linked; wisdom must be more than intellect.

The Heart Sutra, which is chanted daily by many Mahayana Buddhists around the world, communicates emptiness as the heart of understanding. It is the gift of nonfear from Avalokiteshvara, the embodiment of compassion who attends the world's cries for help. The sutra opens with these words:

> The Bodhisattva Avalokita, while moving in the deep course of Perfect Understanding, shed light on the five skandhas and found them equally empty. After this penetration, he overcame all pain.

Thich Nhat Hanh concludes his commentary on this passage in *The Heart of Understanding* this way:

> Avalokita looked deeply into the five skandhas of form, feelings, perceptions, mental formation, and consciousness, and he discovered that none of them can be by itself alone. Each can only inter-be with all the others. So he tells us that form is empty. Form is empty of a separate self, but it is full

of everything in the cosmos. The same is true with feelings, perceptions, mental formations, and consciousness.

The last sentence in this Heart Sutra passage—"After this penetration, he overcame all pain"—is a clear illumination of the words in the Pali Canon concerning the skandhas. The five skandhas—the five collectives: material form, feeling, perception, mental formations, and consciousness—are the sources of dukkha. Fully realizing their emptiness releases one from dukkha.

Although the emphasis of Mahayana teachings on the perfection of wisdom through understanding emptiness differs from that of Theravada, both embrace deep and direct understanding of reality and compassion for all beings.

Wisdom and Livelihood

As we explore transforming our lives into our spiritual practice, one of the most challenging starting arenas is our work life. The big questions are what we do, why we do it, and how we do it, including how we relate to those in our workplace and community. The wisdom of livelihood is to choose an occupation skillfully and to use our skills wisely.

What We Do, and Why

Livelihood usually means how we earn our living, but here our discussion also includes it to mean how we spend most of our time, whether we get paid for it or not.

The *why* of what we do should be simple: to benefit beings, including ourselves. That is, our livelihood should enable us to meet our financial and communal responsibilities. At the same time, it should be a way to manifest our understanding of our spiritual path and allow us to grow in the spiritual role we seek.

The Buddha said in Anguttara Nikaya 5.177 that wise livelihood excludes particular categories of work: "A lay follower should not engage in these five trades. What five? Trading in weapons, trading in living beings, trading in meat, trading in intoxicants, and trading in poisons." If we reflect on these categories, we see that they are all variations on the five precepts and morality. Broadly, we should exclude any forms of livelihood that directly or indirectly cause harm to other beings.

How We Perform Our Livelihood

Wise livelihood has two aspects: what we choose as our livelihood, which we discussed in the previous section, and how we perform it.

Wise intention is critical. If, for example, our goal is to use the energy, determination, and concentration we develop through our spiritual practice to make ever-more money, we are contravening our practice by using it to foster grasping and clinging, the causes of dis-ease. We can use the same heart characteristics of energy, determination, and concentration to improve our ability to work for the benefit of all beings.

Besides listing five careers that are wrong livelihood, the Buddha directly commented, in Majjhima Nikaya 117.29, on what we should avoid doing in the "wise" careers we have chosen: "Scheming, talking, hinting, belittling, pursuing gain with gain: this is wrong livelihood." The five precepts are useful guidelines for how we wisely pursue our livelihood. As many of us have found out, the workplace is sometimes the most challenging situation in which to practice. Let's look briefly at each precept in relationship to livelihood.

1. **To abstain from harming living beings.** It is critical to avoid harming through our choice of livelihood, but it is equally important to avoid acting in ways that harm others as we work. Bringing mindfulness to our daily lives can penetrate the indifference and apathy that allow us to overlook the ways we harm others, often through breaking another precept. In competitive work situations, we must be careful not to have the mean-spirited intention to put others out of business, whether they are people who are coworkers over whom we seek advantage or outside competitors. Here, intention is a key part of harming.

2. **To abstain from taking what is not given freely.** This can be any situation of stealing, from misrepresenting expense accounts, to bringing "extra" toner cartridges or other supplies home, to taking credit for others' work, to taking power away from others as a way of building ourselves up.

3. **To abstain from sexual misconduct.** Sexual misconduct is frequently a way that people take what is not freely given in a work situation. It harms ourselves and families, the person with whom we have illicit relations, and everyone within the workplace.

4. **To abstain from false speech.** Here's where the proscription against "scheming, talking, hinting, belittling" really comes in. Office politics and gossip are terribly destructive to everyone and sometimes are very hard to avoid if we're not vigilant. Abusive speech can harm others, and frivolous speech simply wastes everyone's time.

5. **To abstain from the use of intoxicating substances.** Intoxicants cloud our mindfulness and concentration and interfere with our ability to do our job well, or perhaps at all. Misusing intoxicants also can play a causal role in breaking the other precepts. For example: A drunk operator of a vehicle, ship, or plane can injure others and the environment. A drunk person may be verbally abusive to employees or may steal from the company to cover financial losses resulting from substance abuse. Intoxicants often are contributing factors to sexual misconduct, whether an indiscretion at an office party or beginning a longer-term affair.

Many long-term spiritual practitioners have become increasingly aware of how committing to live by the precepts affects their life in the workplace. In some cases, it has affected the kind of work chosen or abandoned; people have gone into helping professions or some type of career that enables them to work for the benefit of all beings. In our work life, under difficult circumstances where we refuse to play the game of unskillful actions, we can even get fired. Cultivating wisdom and the other perfections changes our relationship to everything we do in all aspects of our lives.

Practice and Reflection: Wisdom

1. A derogatory way of referring to someone who is ignorant is "That person only has one oar in the water." How do you think that mental acumen that isn't accompanied by compassion is like having one oar in the water?

2. Compare two truisms in terms of the perfection of wisdom: "Happiness is wanting what you have" and artist Jenny Holzer's "Protect me from what I want."

3. Do you believe that it is possible to pursue enduring happiness for both oneself and others at the same time? Why or why not? How or how not?

4. Does your source of livelihood—including investments and retirement funds—harm anyone? If you discovered they do, would you change these sources to ones that are nonharming? Why or why not?

5. Do you ever take what is not freely given from your workplace? Things? Money? Credit? Power? Does one kind of taking feel more acceptable than another? Why or why not?

6. Have you had a flirtation or illicit sexual relationship in your workplace? How did it feel at the time? How did it feel afterward?

7. Do you get pulled into office gossip? If so, how do you feel during and afterward? If not, do others treat you differently (with mistrust or respect) as a result? What is the most difficult speech concern for you in the workplace?

8. Have you ever been intoxicated in a work situation? If so, did you feel regret afterward? Have you ever lost a job or promotion because of substance abuse? Have you ever broken one of the other precepts while intoxicated?

9. Have you ever changed jobs or careers as the result of coming to understand wise livelihood?

10. Sit quietly for ten minutes and do a meditation practice using the repetition of these phrases as the object of your concentration/mindfulness. As you silently repeat the phrases, do so slowly enough to feel what each one would be like in your life:

> May I be happy.
> May I be healthy.
> May I live in safety.
> May my choices be wise and compassionate.

10.
Wise Effort

Resolution: May I awaken and sustain the perfections in my life.

Mantra: May goodness energize my life.

Moderation

WHEN WE THINK about undertaking a spiritual path, we rarely consider such daily activities as brushing our teeth or going for regular medical checkups to be important parts of that journey. Yet the amount of effort we put into sustaining skillful life habits is as critical a part of the path as the effort we put into awakening. The trick is to attune the level of energy to our personal needs and maintain that level—not too much, not too little, but the skillful amount. Learning how to take care of ourselves with care and moderation is part of the stewardship we assume in taking care of others in our immediate relationships. The Buddha made the point about how important it is first to take care of ourselves as part of taking care of others in a tale about two acrobats:

One acrobat asks his assistant, "Frying Pan," to stand on his shoulders. She does, and he says, "Now you watch after me, my dear Frying Pan, and I'll watch after you. Thus, protecting one another, watching after one another, we'll show off our skill, receive our reward, and come down safely from the bamboo pole."

But Frying Pan disagrees and responds, "But that won't do at all,

Master. You watch after yourself, and I'll watch after myself, and thus with each of us protecting ourselves, watching after ourselves, we'll show off our skill, receive our reward, and come down safely from the bamboo pole."

The Buddha added to this story: "Monks, a foundation of mindfulness is to be practiced with the thought 'I'll watch after myself.' A foundation of mindfulness is to be practiced with the thought 'I'll watch after others.' When watching after oneself, one watches after others. When watching after others, one watches after oneself."

We come to see that self care is necessary because we can't care for others if we ourselves are infirm. In small personal acts we extend this self care; for example, you might buy a good-quality moisturizer if your hands crack and bleed in the winter, not just because you're worried about wrinkles.

At a study group recently, a friend commented that she found the concept of moderation in daily life to be totally elusive. It didn't matter what she was doing—in this case, planting a vegetable garden twice as big as she could take care of—she always seemed to overdo. As the group began to talk about moderation, several points became clear: Moderation is often the greatest challenge—at least in that group—in relationship to physical activity, such as skiing or gardening, and to eating specific foods, especially chocolate and ice cream. Immoderation (greed) leads to dis-ease, whether aching muscles, sugar shock, or weight gain. Acknowledging the inevitable dis-ease following immoderation led us to explore more deeply how greed, clinging, and attachment in such a seemingly wholesome pursuit as gardening is still greed, clinging, and attachment.

I had a very unpleasant example of this several years ago. I decided to plant bulbs in a large section of my garden. I laid everything out "perfectly," so the heights of plants increased toward the back, blooming season varied from row to row, and colors were dramatically alternated. I dug the ideal hole and put some bone meal in each one before carefully putting in and burying the bulbs. The next morning, my flowerbed was a disaster, with bulbs strewn all over the yard. It seems that skunks find bone meal to be ambrosia and had dug up every single bulb and tossed it away to get at the bone meal. At first I was devastated—all my hard work was for naught. But eventually I saw the futility in resenting hungry animals. I no longer knew what any bulb was, so I just poked them into the ground wherever they lay—even in the middle of other beds—watered them, and let them be. Every spring now I have a glorious display of surprises, more aesthetic than my careful planning could have ever created.

Dis-ease does not fester in an object or activity by itself but in how we relate to that object or activity. The Buddha-to-be learned that this lesson can be found in relationship to the pursuit of just about everything, including sensual pleasures and even spirituality.

Siddhartha Gautama, by the standards of his time, was raised in considerable luxury. His father was the head of the Sakya clan and had three grand residences, for hot weather, for cold weather, and for rainy weather. Cloth for Siddartha's clothing was purchased from the finest makers in Varanasi, and he was surrounded by beautiful young women to serve and entertain him. But this luxury did not outweigh his personal response to his first encounters with old age, illness, death, and a spiritual seeker; Siddhartha became disillusioned with his life of excess and went on his own spiritual quest. From opulence, he went to the opposite extreme and lived in conditions of severe austerity as an ascetic. But after several years of deprivation, he realized that this path of deprivation was bringing him no closer to the understanding he sought. It was similar to the experience of many adults who achieve their lifelong dream and find themselves asking, "Is this all there is?"

One day while still living as an ascetic, Siddhartha recalled an experience he had had as a child: During a festival he had sat in deep meditation and discovered a peace greater than he had ever experienced. He realized that deep meditative absorption was the way to understanding but that he could not achieve this state while he was as weak and emaciated as he was from his severe asceticism. In Samyutta Nikaya 56.11, he recounts his realization this way:

These two extremes should not be followed by one who has gone forth into homelessness. What two? The pursuit of sensual happiness in sensual pleasures, which is low, vulgar, the way of worldlings, ignoble, unbeneficial; and the pursuit of self-mortification, which is painful, ignoble, unbeneficial. Without veering toward either of these extremes, the Tathagata has awakened to the middle way, which gives rise to vision, which gives rise to knowledge, which leads to peace, to direct knowledge, to enlightenment, to Nibbana.

The middle way between extremes is the Noble Eightfold Path, but it is also a prescription for how to live our lives in terms of the effort or energy we put into pursuing the path.

Perfecting Wise Effort

Dhammapala defines the perfection of wise effort as mental and physical work for the welfare of others undertaken with compassion and skillful means. He stresses that in the fostering of the perfections, energy is immediately after wisdom for the following reasons:

1. The function of wisdom is perfected by the arousing of energy.
2. To show the miraculous work a buddha-to-be undertakes for the welfare of beings.
3. To state the causal basis for exertion right after the basis for equanimity to support the knowledge of the reason for moderation.
4. To demonstrate that wise effort must be applied right after the activity of careful consideration; first we must reflect in wisdom, then we must act.

Directing Our Energy to Four Goals

In Samyutta Nikaya 45.8, the Buddha gave very specific directions as to where we should apply this wise, balanced, and tuned effort. It should be applied in four areas: nonarising of unwholesome states, abandoning of unwholesome states that have already arisen, desire for the arising of wholesome states, and desire for maintenance of wholesome states. In other words, a person seeks good states and avoids bad ones, just as he or she cultivates other good qualities.

In sum, we are to use our energy to renounce unwholesome states before and after they arise; we are to cultivate wholesome states before and after ("maintaining") they arise. To meet these goals, we invoke the teachings of the Eightfold Path. We abandon wrong understanding, wrong intention, wrong speech, wrong action, and wrong livelihood, and we put our tuned and balanced effort into cultivating and implementing wise understanding, wise intention, wise speech, wise action, and wise livelihood.

When I think of energy as avoiding or renouncing unwholesome states and unskillful qualities, and cultivating and maintaining wholesome states and skillful qualities, I am reminded of the law of conservation of energy in the natural sciences: energy can be transformed but not created or destroyed. In our use of wise energy then, we can transform the causes of suffering into the causes of happiness. With wise understanding of suffering, its cause, and its end; of impermanence; of karma; of not-self, we can commit our lives to the intention of nonharming through our thoughts, words, and actions. We strengthen mindfulness and concentration to support and implement these intentions. Such understanding arouses in us the energy and sense of spiritual urgency to develop heart-mind characteristics such as the perfections. So far, this book has tended to stress compassion and liberation for all beings, without specifically pointing out that we are among those beings. It's more than appropriate at this point to put the focus of these skillful efforts on ourselves.

The Four Efforts in Taking Care of Ourselves

There are infinite examples of how the efforts to eliminate unskillful qualities and cultivate skillful qualities play out in our lives.

One broad study could be how we take care of ourselves physically, mentally, and spiritually on an ongoing, daily basis. With wisdom and mindfulness, we can develop the energy we need to pursue our spiritual path. How we use this energy depends upon how able-bodied we are. Even if we are bedridden we can have a consistent meditation practice and involve ourselves with Dharma issues on the telephone and Internet.

Another important part of wisdom is understanding just how precious and rare human birth is. Here's how the Buddha described this rarity to his disciples, in Samyutta Nikaya 56.48:

> Suppose that this great earth had become one mass of water, and a man would throw a yoke with a single hole upon it... There was a blind turtle which would come to the surface once every hundred years. What do you think, would that blind turtle, coming to the surface once every hundred years, insert its neck into that yoke with a single hole?

At first the parable of a blind turtle rising once every hundred years to accidentally poke its head through a yoke may seem an exaggerated depiction of the infrequency of human birth. When we think only of human beings, the earth seems crowded, but when we consider the billions of other life forms—including insects—we can get a sense of how extremely unusual our being born human is.

When we realize how truly rare and precious this gift of human life is, we are moved to honor and take care of it. When we look toward taking care of ourselves, it is helpful to check ourselves out physically and in our heart-minds—to literally take an inventory of what there is too much of or too little of on our personal shelf. The key factor in working with all four of these efforts is mindfulness of our intentions, words, and actions.

In the following sections are checklists comparable to those used for maintenance servicing of vehicles. Take the time to go through each list and see whether or not you're in skillful "working order." The number of questions may seem daunting. These lists are meant to be reminders of possibilities rather than complex rulebooks for putting our lives in boot camp. Simply look at the questions periodically and see if you are missing any opportunities for enriching your spiritual life.

Guarding Against Unarisen Unwholesome States

In Western culture, lessons about "guarding" tend to be given quite early to most children: "Brush your teeth." "Wash your hands before you eat." "Get vaccinations to prevent childhood diseases." "Cross streets only when the light is green." Much modeling behavior is given when we're quite young and sets up hygiene and safety habits for a lifetime. As we age, we modify the early habits as appropriate: We get "regular," prophylactic dental checkups. We wash our hands after using the toilet and before meals, but also frequently when there are colds and flu in our household. We look before crossing intersections but also drive defensively when conditions warrant. Some of us get flu or pneumonia vaccines or use herbal remedies to prevent illness.

As we grow older, we also become increasingly aware of more complex and subtle ways we need to "protect" ourselves. "Clean up your room" becomes the groundwork for implementing the cleanliness practices that will keep our homes and property free from ants, cockroaches, mice, and other germ-bearing critters. We use clothing or sunblock to prevent those sunburns many of us once thought looked so healthy. We have our automobiles serviced regularly to avoid adding to pollution and to improve mileage.

Here are some other ways we can inventory how well we are guarding ourselves from the arising of unwholesome states:

Physical
1. Do I avoid becoming overtired by regularly getting enough sleep or resting when I need to?
2. Do I dress warmly or coolly enough for the seasonal temperature? Do I wear a hat for warmth or to prevent overexposure to the sun?

3. Do I always wear sunblock or covering clothing when the sun is strong in the summer or when I am doing winter sports?

4. Do I wear suitable shoes for my activity level?

5. Do I have routine medical examinations, including mammograms, pap tests, or prostrate-cancer screening, as frequently as recommended for someone my age?

Heart-Mind

1. Do I plan into my life the time for leisure activities such as reading, going to lectures, or taking courses?

2. Do I avoid, as much as possible, spending time with negative people who can pull me into emotionally stressful situations?

3. Do I avoid indulging in self-pity, self-criticism, and other negative ways of reinforcing a sense of self?

4. Do I avoid unwise speech, such as gossip, and action, such as driving recklessly?

5. Do I avoid situations that violate the five precepts and cause remorse?

6. Do I make time for daily meditation?

7. Do I try to see reality as it is or do I escape through overdoing or sleeping or eating to avoid unpleasant aspects?

8. Do I ever set aside the time to check myself against the four foundations of mindfulness to get a sense of how I am doing spiritually?

Abandoning Arisen Unwholesome States

A great challenge for many of us is to have the wisdom to slash through delusion so that we can actually see our unskillful qualities. So often these unskillful qualities are simply habits—the way we've always lived or thought or worked. When we focus the light of awareness on *all* our intentions, words, and actions and can honestly ask whether they lead to dis-ease for ourselves or others, we can then direct our effort to abandoning those that cause harm. The wisdom of insight will arouse the spiritual urgency and energy to abandon those unskillful qualities.

Physical

1. Do you break up long periods of sedentary behavior with physical activity such as taking walks?
2. Do you overeat, or eat unwisely?
3. Do you overindulge in food or intoxicants?
4. Do you drive when you have used intoxicants?
5. Do you use more than your fair share of natural resources by doing things like taking long showers or driving a low-mileage vehicle?
6. Do you assert "your" rights as an aggressive car driver?
7. Do you kill insects?

Heart-Mind

1. Do you hold on to resentments?
2. Do you indulge in sexual fantasies?
3. Do you feel pity rather than compassion for less fortunate people?
4. Do you indulge in "justifiable anger" when you consider political issues?
5. Do you think you're better than other people? Different?
6. Do you maintain that the end justifies any means?

Developing Unarisen Wholesome States

This category of effort is the grown-up version of New Year's resolutions. The first stage is to decide the kind of person you want to become, remembering the preciousness of the human life entrusted to you—a person whose life benefits and does not harm self and others. As you consider what you wish to develop, it's important not to program yourself to failure by unrealistically laying out more than you can accomplish at once. Take the middle path and get to become that person by successive approximations on everything, except outright harming.

Physical

1. Have I established a regular exercise plan appropriate to my health and age?

2. Do I plan meals for variety, nutrition, and weight control?
3. Do I have regular times to go to bed and to get up?
4. Have I set aside regular times for leisure activities?
5. If I have any physical limitations, have I set up a way to deal with them as effectively as possible through physical therapy, acupuncture, Feldenkrais work, chiropractic, or activities such as swimming or weight training under the direction of a professional?

Heart-Mind

1. Have I set up a specific time each day for meditation or reflection?
2. Have I systematically studied key Dharma teachings such as the Four Noble Truths/Eightfold Path, the five precepts, the three refuges, the perfections, the Brahmaviharas?

Maintaining Arisen Wholesome States

Maintaining skillful qualities developed on the foundation of wisdom is the product of intention and mindfulness. Sometimes it is helpful to establish some "mindfulness bells" to punctuate our day with clear and focused awareness. For example, I assign the function of arousing my mindfulness to the following events: the ringing of the telephone, the hourly birdsongs of my Audubon clock, brakelights on the car in front of me when I'm driving, any time my hands touch water. In these instances, I pause, take three deep breaths, and make sure I am in the present moment with mindfulness.

1. Do I practice mindfulness meditation every day?
2. Have I assigned "mindfulness bell" status to some ordinary events of my daily life?
3. Do I eat mindfully during one meal or a portion of one meal a day by noticing texture and taste of food? Or do I eat a whole meal caught up in conversation or reading or watching TV and not taste any of it?
4. Do I exercise mindfully, paying attention to each movement in the same way as when doing walking meditation?

5. Am I mindful during daily hygiene activities such as brushing my teeth and bathing?

6. Is my lifework compatible with wise livelihood in terms of not harming but benefitting others?

7. Do I regularly meet with a sangha or "spiritual friends" with whom I can discuss my spiritual goals?

8. Do I have opportunity for continuity of practice by attending silent meditation retreats or doing mindfulness self-retreats, perhaps for one day a month?

The Three Refuges as a Source of Energy

Besides these "energy inventories" above, I have found one daily practice that gives me the motivation and energy to dedicate my life to living by the Buddha's teachings. This practice is a daily answer to the question "Why am I doing this anyway?" The simple practice is daily recitation of and reflection on the three refuges, repeated three times:

> I go for refuge to the Buddha.
> I go for refuge to the Dharma.
> I go for refuge to the Sangha.

Originally, if people wanted to formally become disciples of the Buddha, they knelt before a previously ordained monk and repeated the three refuges three times. The term *Buddha* referred to the historic person born as Siddhartha Gautama. The *Dharma* was the teachings of the Buddha. The *Sangha* was the ordained community who followed the Buddha.

These are still the basic meanings of the refuges, but many of us, through reflection, have expanded their connotations. For example, the Buddha showed us what is possible, and repeating his name reminds me what is possible for me in this lifetime and that I have within me "buddha nature" that I can actualize.

The *Dharma* still refers to the Buddha's teachings, but for me the term also refers to truth. The Buddha did not invent truth. Truth is truth. He merely articulated truth in a way that has been accessible to those who have chosen to embrace it. The purpose of insight meditation is to see the world as it really is, and the way it really is the Dharma, which is piece by piece revealed to those of us who mindfully pursue it.

The *Sangha* is the ordained disciples of the Buddha, but for many of us it is also the specific spiritual group with whom we practice or even the worldwide community of spiritual seekers. Because of the interconnectedness of all life, some of us believe that all living beings are our world sangha.

Vipassana teacher Arinna Weisman has offered wording for the refuges that reflects these connotations:

> May I take refuge in my capacity to awaken.
> May I take refuge in the ways of living that bring about my freedom and happiness.
> May I take refuge in those who are fully awakened and feel open to all those who can support me on this path of freedom.

An acquaintance of mine who is an anonymous alcoholic in recovery recites the refuges this way:

> I go for refuge to the Buddha, to my own possibility for freedom and happiness as long as I do not drink.
> I go for refuge to the Dharma, the possibility to see what is real and true in sobriety.
> I go for refuge to the Sangha, to my interconnectedness with all beings and especially in fellowship with other sober alcoholics.

When I was on a metta retreat some years ago, I found I was integrating the practice of taking the refuges with metta practice, with these meanings:

> Taking refuge in the Buddha: loving myself.
> Taking refuge in the Dharma: seeing myself clearly.
> Taking refuge in the Sangha: honoring myself in all other beings.

Although I use the traditional phrases as part of my daily practice, my reflections on the meanings vary from day to day, from situation to situation, depending upon what's going on in my life. But no matter what contexts arise for me, I find that the simple act of taking refuge gives remarkably supportive energy, even spiritual urgency, to my practice.

Practice and Reflection: Energy

1. In what activities is it most difficult for you to practice moderation—the middle path—in daily life? Why?

2. In what activities do you experience the lowest energy? The highest energy? Why?

3. How much influence do your attitudes have in terms of having enough energy to do tasks you may sometimes find unattractive, such as housekeeping or going to the office? Does understanding why such tasks must be accomplished help you to muster the energy to do them?

4. What are the most personally challenging unskillful qualities, intentions, words, and actions you must guard against?

5. What are the most personally challenging unskillful qualities, intentions, words, and actions you must abandon?

6. What are the most personally important skillful qualities, intentions, words, and actions you must develop?

7. What are the most personally important skillful qualities, intentions, words, and actions you must maintain?

8. When you experience stress, where do you go for refuge?

For example, to family, or to nature, or to the movies? Can you relate your "refuge of choice" to any of the three refuges?

9. When you go for refuge to the Buddha, the Dharma, and the Sangha, what does each of these terms mean to your heart-mind?

10. Sit quietly for ten minutes and do a meditation practice using the repetition of these phrases as the object of your concentration/mindfulness. As you silently repeat the phrases, do so slowly enough to feel what each one would be like in your life:

May I be happy.
May I be healthy.
May I live in safety.
May goodness energize my life.

11.
Patience

Resolution: May I be patient and forgiving when self-centered fear or anger arises, accepting things just as they are.

Mantra: May I be patient and forgiving to all.

WHEN EARLY SCHOLARS were trying to trace the development of the perfections in the Buddha, they often turned to the Jataka Tales, those early stories of the past lives of the Buddha-to-be. These stories show many aspects of the Buddha's evolution, including the patience needed during many, many lifetimes in many realms, challenged by Mara at every turn. One of the most popular stories for understanding patience, and its relationship to karma, involves a buffalo and a monkey.

Once upon a time, the Buddha was born as a great and strong buffalo who roamed the Himalayas. One day as he stood in the shade of a pleasant tree eating, an impertinent monkey jumped down onto his back and voided excrement all over the buffalo, then swung from his horns and kept on harassing the buffalo each time he returned to this tree. Finally, the sprite that belonged to this tree (there were usually sprites in Jataka Tales, and they often spoke in verse) came out and chided the buffalo for putting up with such demeaning behavior. In Dhammapala's phrasing in *Treatise on the Paramis*:

"Why do you patiently endure each freak
This mischievous and selfish ape may wreak?
Crush underfoot and transfix him with your horn!
Stop him or even children will show scorn."

The Buddha replied that if he could not endure this monkey's ill-treatment, how could he ever develop and purify the qualities for enlightenment? Some other would destroy the evil monkey, and he, the buffalo, would "be delivered both from pain and from blood-guiltiness."

The key lesson here is expressed in the words "I shall be delivered both from pain and from blood-guiltiness." Implied in this story are some major characteristics of patience. First, by purifying patience, the buffalo preserved his own karmic integrity by not harming another being. Second, the most common challenge to patience is anger, and patience is expressed as perseverance in the face of insult. Anger is the greatest threat to mindfulness and our ability to cultivate the perfections. Anger is the gap between what is and what we want the world to be—which is one of the Buddha's definitions of dis-ease. Most often, anger arises from some form of self-centered fear: fear of being abandoned or rejected, of not getting what we want, of losing what we want and have. Learning patience in these situations is learning to be truthful to ourselves about the exact nature of reality and giving ourselves the time to deal slowly with it. Sometimes we are quite blind to our own anger and impatience.

Several years ago, Marcia Rose, a teacher whom I was going to assist at a retreat, suggested that I give two talks on the perfections. I said, "Fine. How about the first two, generosity and morality?" She recommended instead that I talk about generosity and patience. I later told her how much I appreciated those suggestions, that I had especially enjoyed doing the research on patience, which was a wonderful topic because it is so rarely talked about. She smiled and replied, "That isn't why I wanted *you* to spend some time thinking about patience."

She really caught me! When I was growing up, I often heard the aphorism "Patience is a virtue." That sentiment baffled me. I was an immediate-gratification type from the get-go, and my favorite cartoon showed a group of protesters carrying signs that read: *Patience Now!* My impatience has moderated somewhat with the passing years, but Marcia was right on target when she said I needed to focus more on patience.

It is not possible to develop a meditation practice without also developing patience. Patience can be specifically worked with, but if we are meditating in our spiritual practice, it sneaks up on us anyway. My first clue to this amazing manifestation was when I realized that I had begun *responding* rather than *reacting* to events in my life. Between the thought or intention and the word or action there was a calming moment that I realized was patience.

The need for patience is clearly projected by the Four Noble Truths. The nature of life is that there is unavoidable stress or suffering, from a broken wheel on a shopping cart to the death of a loved one. Each experience of dis-ease has an origin, an end, and a way to that end. The events are going to come whether we want them or not, and the amount of suffering we experience depends upon our relationship to the circumstance or event. Here's where patience comes in. When we immerse ourselves in these teachings, we learn some important things about dis-ease—such as that it's not personal to us (it happens to everyone) and that it is impermanent (it will pass). These two truths can unlock the door of patience for us.

Dhammapala pinpoints key aspects of patience in his *Treatise on the Paramis*. He highlights qualities of patience this way:

> The perfection of patience is the endurance of harm imposed by beings and formations, or the act of consciousness occurring in such a mode, predominated by non-aversion and accompanied by compassion and skillful means...
>
> Patience has the characteristic of acceptance; its function is to endure the desirable and undesirable; its manifestation is tolerance or non-opposition; seeing things as they really are is its proximate cause...

Patience is the unimpeded weapon of the good in the development of noble qualities, for it dispels anger, the opposite of all such qualities, without residue...

Patience should be further strengthened by reflecting... "Although this suffering arises through the wrong deeds of others, this body of mine is the field for that suffering, and the action which is its seed was sown by me alone." And: "This suffering will release me from the debt of that kamma." And: "If there were no wrong-doers, how could I accomplish the perfection of patience?"

When we begin to work specifically with the qualities of patience, its very special gifts begin almost immediately to manifest. We can see the need to back down from the anger that tends to arise first, then we can open more to the jewel of patience. I can see more clearly that my karma and the karma of the person who is challenging me are inextricably linked, making clear the need to keep my karma "clean" if I am to develop spiritually. When I am working specifically with patience, I personally find that my intentions and path are clearer than when I work with other perfections. I also find patience the most difficult to refine, given its relationship to anger.

Anger

In most of his tales and discourses, the Buddha talked about patience as being the antidote to anger and stressed its value especially in warfare and other kinds of conflict.

In Samutta Nikaya 11.4, the *Vepacitti Sutta*, or *Patience Sutta*, the Buddha clearly laid out the virtue in being patient. Vepacitti, the lord of the demons, lost in battle to Sakka, the lord of the heavenly beings. Vepacitti was brought to Sakka and began to abuse him verbally. Sakka's charioteer questioned Sakka's enduring this abuse, and Sakka replied, in a number of verses:

It is neither through fear nor weakness
That I am patient with Vepacitti.
How can a wise person like me
Engage in combat with a fool?...

Of goals that culminate in one's own good
None is found better than patience.

When a person endowed with strength
Patiently endures a weakling,
They call that the supreme patience;
The weakling must be patient always...

[The patient one] practices for the welfare of both,
His own and the other's,
When knowing that his foe is angry,
He mindfully maintains his peace.

Throughout many teachings the Buddha referred directly and indirectly to the role patience plays in preparation for combat, but always present is the truth that patience has its greatest impact on our own and the other's karma.

As later scholars reexamined the perfections, one of the classic early works in the Mahayana tradition was the eighth-century monk Shantideva's *Guide to the Bodhisattva's Way of Life*. This work cites patience along with meditative concentration as *the* key factors on the path to buddhahood. Shantideva speaks of patience as the key antidote to anger, the experience that most often derails us from this path:

1. Good works gathered in a thousand ages,
Such as deeds of generosity,
Or offerings to the Blissful Ones—
A single flash of anger shatters them.
2. No evil is there similar to hatred,

Nor austerity to be compared with patience.
Steep yourself therefore in patience
In all ways, urgently, with zeal...
7. Getting what I do not want
And that which hinders my desire—
There my mind finds fuel for misery,
Anger springs from it and beats me down...
14. There is nothing that does not
Grow easier through habit.
Putting up with little troubles
Will enable me to endure much sorrow.

We have all experienced what happens to us when we are going through a lovely phase of equanimity and something pricks our anger. We blow up and out. Getting angry under such circumstances, according to Shantideva, is like getting angry at a fire for its heat or a sky for its clouds. As is always true when we're cultivating patience, the "wrongdoer" is in fact a benefactor who teaches us patience and compassion.

Anger is relational. We most often feel angry in relation to another person, or sometimes to ourselves. When we have enough patience for clear thought, our entire attitude toward whatever is making us angry changes: seeing and thinking clearly is the key goal and fruit of patience. When we learn the patience to give ourselves time before reacting, all of the Buddha's teachings come into play. We see the Noble Truths of the existence, cause, and end of suffering, for without the stress of suffering we wouldn't need patience; we cultivate acceptance, endurance, tolerance, and compassion.

A great way to cultivate patience is to reflect on patience and anger. When we do so, we can see suffering clearly, we can see karma, we can see impermanence and not-self, and we can see the benefits of patience in not taking actions. We learn that patience and forbearance are not weaknesses but strengths. We have many contexts for this practice: driving, learning a new skill, training a puppy, waiting for water to boil at high altitude, gardening, and especially in our meditation practice at home and on retreats. Stillness comes when it does, insight comes when it does, monkey mind stops when it does, physical discomfort comes and goes when it does. Learning to abide with these elements when we sit and develop meditative absorption is a terrific way to learn to abide with the greater sufferings when they come.

The Buddha relates the woes of impatience in a Jataka tale about the king of Kosala, who had set out to start a war during a very inhospitable season. In this story, the Buddha tells the king about an owl who went into a thicket of bamboo and hid there from a flock of crows who were out to get the owl. The owl was impatient and did not wait for darkness before it came out. When the owl tried to escape, the crows set upon it and killed it. The king asked the Buddha why the crows attacked, and the Buddha answered that the owl left home before its time. E. B. Cowell's edition of the tale shows the result of untimely efforts:

> There is a time for every thing: who forth from home will go
> One man or many, out of time, will surely meet some woe;
> As did the owl, unlucky fowl, pecked dead by many a crow.
> The king went back home, rather than go to war.

Not too many of us will be set upon by crows for our impatience. But the karmic fruits of our impatience can have broad effects on others as well as ourselves. A mantra for patience could be: "Give yourself time."

Patience with Pets and Children

One of the clearest ways we can see the effect of anger and impatience is by looking to those with whom we share our lives, human and otherwise.

Anger has clear ripples that affect those around us, as it plays out through karma. As Dhammapala put it: "Those who lack patience are afflicted in this world and apply themselves to actions which will lead to their affliction in the life to come." That includes the life to come of others around them. It is well documented that most adults who abuse their children were themselves abused by their parents. Seeing the results of our lack of patience with our children may take decades, but because pets' lives are shorter, we can see the results of impatience and anger upon them much more immediately.

Let's look first at a few examples of what can happen while training a puppy. My dog, Sophie, is an Affenpinscher—a breed that is intelligent, sensitive, sassy, protective and loyal, and as willful as any two-year-old child. She has been a great teacher of patience. Whenever anyone comes to the door, she barks. In her mind she is doing her job. Her sense of the territory she has to protect has expanded geometrically, and she wants to bark at everyone who walks by on the way to the nearby library. Early on, in frustration at her barking, I yelled at her, "No bark!" She thought *I* was barking too and barked even louder at the passersby and at me. I've learned that if I whisper to her and touch her lightly to get her attention, she doesn't bark. At least when I'm there... When I'm away, she still guards the house, loudly.

I got Sophie when she was five months old. Before she came to me, she had been able to go outside freely whenever she wanted to relieve herself or play with other dogs who lived there. The day she arrived, she pooped on my rare Turkish rug. When I discovered the pile some time later, I exploded and loudly told her how bad she was. She had no idea what she had done wrong and went away and hid from my wrath. Her breeder suggested that I train her to ring a bell when she needed to go out by putting peanut butter on a suspended bell near the door and taking her out each time she (accidentally) rang the bell. It took less than two days for me to train her to ring the bell when she needed to go out. It took her about another two days to train me to take her out when she *wanted* to go out— whether she needed to or not—especially when the neighbor's orange cat paraded by with tail straight up. When I was patient with Sophie, she did eventually learn not to lie about her needs but to communicate clearly. Most of the time, anyway—when skunks come around at night, she rings the bell frantically, howls, and does the tango.

Because Sophie is small, and we walk on fairly deserted public sidewalks in the small town where I live, I didn't train Sophie to "heel" and walk tightly at my side. After all, it's her walk, so I got an extendable leash, and I let her wander around and sniff at her own pace. On an early walk, she tugged at the leash a lot, and at one point lunged toward a particularly odiferous dead something that she wanted to roll in. I jerked on the leash and yelled, "No!" She jerked back, planted her feet, and pulled even harder. And barked at me. With patience, I learned to encourage her to look back at me frequently (by softly calling her name), checking in, and to come my way when I gently say, "This way... good girl."

Nevertheless, patience in training a puppy does not mean letting the puppy do whatever she wants to, whenever she wants to. For happiness in shared space, she has learned what's expected of her. For safety's sake, I have taught her two sharp commands: "Sit" and "Come." But I speak these commands not in anger, just firmly, like alpha dog, a role important for me to maintain with an Affenpinscher. In these three puppy-training areas, I've learned to teach with patience, which has led to a wonderful closeness. She knows what is expected of her, and she meets these expectations with a silly grin and a wagging tail.

In raising children, the same patience is needed. I do not have children of my own but I have been close to others' children, and I certainly had the experience of being a child and remember quite well how some of my parents' childrearing practices affected me.

California meditation teacher Gil Fronsdal retells a dramatic Jataka Tale of a parent learning patience. In this story, the parent was a stepmother, whose stepson took an immediate dislike to her and fought with her about everything. The stepmother went to the local shaman and asked if there were a way to solve this problem. The shaman answered, "Certainly. But first you must bring me three whiskers from a lion." The woman was quite taken aback by this request but felt that establishing a good relationship with her stepson was worth any difficulty she had to go through. She began to go to a nearby forest where a large male lion was known to hang out. At first and for many weeks, she just stood silently at a safe distance. Over time she began to move closer, and finally she would bring food for the lion, put it down, then back away. Gradually she stayed closer and closer, until one day after eating, the lion lay down beside her and fell asleep. She plucked the three whiskers and was about to take them to the shaman when she realized this was not necessary: She had already learned all the patience she needed to deal with a difficult child.

One of the most amazing opportunities we may have is to observe language acquisition in a child. When we are patient and warmly acknowledge successive approximations to real words, children's learning to speak is an unfolding miracle. But when parents express anger and frustration to children verbally, the children respond in kind, with crying or yelling or sullen withdrawal. Children raised by parents who yell at them in anger are likely to "bark" at their children the same way. As the Bible says, "A soft answer turns away wrath"; when we are calm and soft-spoken with our children, their karmic inheritance is more likely to be the same.

In housebreaking a puppy, it's important to take the puppy out when there is the greatest likelihood that it will relieve itself—when it wakes up, shortly after a meal, or shortly after active play—and to reward the puppy verbally and with pats when it is "good." The same thing is true with children. Give children the opportunity to be "good" by putting them on the potty when it is most likely that they need to relieve themselves, leaving them there long enough (but not in a punishing way), and rewarding them verbally and with hugs when they "perform." When parents get angry with very young children for "making mistakes" and soiling themselves, the children are often baffled at first but come to associate natural functions such as bowel movements with their parents' anger. This association can be the source of dis-ease between the parents and children well into the future.

Animals get to know their world through their senses. For dogs, the primary sense is scent, and allowing them to explore with their noses—within reasonable and safe bounds—is developmentally important to them. Human children too need to explore with their senses, all of them. In terms of movement, the challenge for parents is to create a "safe context" in which children can discover their world. Parents must be extremely mindful in creating this safe space—assuming that many of the objects will end up in the young one's mouth—and extremely patient in letting the young one learn at his or her own pace what this world is about.

As children get older, in frustration we sometimes wish they could learn from our mistakes. And sometimes they can. But what they can learn from us is both our skillful and our unskillful behaviors. If we want children who are happy, loving, and equanimous, we must model those qualities for them, not anger and frustration, which they learn just as readily.

One way parents can plant the karmic seeds of skillful qualities in children is to allow them to have a pet, appropriate for whatever their life situation is. In the beginning, parents can "coparent" the pet, encouraging their children to take more and more responsibility for its well-being. In this role, the parents can model patience, compassion, concern, and affection for their children's future with their own children.

Practice and Reflection: Patience

1. If you are meeting someone at a theater and the person does not arrive on time, do you wait patiently? If the person is habitually late, is your response the same as it is if the person is usually early? What accounts for the difference? Can you use knowledge of whatever underlies the difference to strengthen your general patience?

2. Dhammapala says that patience follows energy in the list of perfections for several reasons, including that energy enables us to be patient and endure "suffering imposed by beings and formations" and to endure the suffering created by others even as we work for their welfare. Do you need energy to be patient?

3. Can you cultivate skillful qualities if you do not have patience?

4. If you have had pets, have you found that you are more patient with animals or with people? Why? Does the kind of pet—dog, cat, bird, horse—affect your level of patience?

5. This book often uses the metaphor of seeds for karmic actions. Reflect on the complex care necessary when you plant (real) seeds and raise a plant. Are you patient with the maturation process, or does it frustrate you that you have to wait so long for some plants to flower or bear fruit? Is the same true when you try to teach another being (human or pet) good manners or a particular skill?

6. What kinds of situations test your patience the most:

- People blowing their horns in traffic jams?

- An angry person yelling at you? What if the anger is "justified"?

- People who take more than their share of natural resources, such as watering their lawn during a drought?

- People who take more than their share of a special dish at a meal so that there is not enough for everyone?

- People who lie to you about their age? About their whereabouts? About their health? About anything at all?

- People who take from you what is not freely given, whether stealing time or stealing attention or stealing objects?

- People who harm other beings?

- Drunk drivers?

- People who abuse their "positions of power" and sexually take advantage of others?

- People who put you down in front of others?

- Neighbors who have gatherings but don't invite you?

7. Pick the annoyance in the bulleted list above that most tries your patience, and reflect on why it is so annoying to you.

8. Sit quietly for ten minutes and do a meditation practice using the repetition of these phrases as the object of your concentration/mindfulness. As you silently repeat the phrases, do so slowly enough to feel what each one would be like in your life:

> May I be happy.
> May I be healthy.
> May I live in safety.
> May I be patient and forgiving to all.

12.
Truthfulness

Resolution: May I be truthful with myself so that there is
harmony between what I say, what I do, and
who I am.

Mantra: May I be truthful with myself and others.

THIS WHOLE BOOK is about "walking the talk"—but we need to focus on *talking* the talk too.

At no time is talking the talk truthfully more important than when we're talking to *ourselves*. There's a critical step since we don't end where we started on our journey that begins with truthfulness, which leads to mindfulness, which leads to resolution, which results in spiritual growth. As we've noted, we must be mindful to note what perfections or imperfections are present at any time, and in order to know whether these are qualities we should cultivate or abandon, we must see them for what they are. We must be honest with ourselves to make this determination. And we surely must be honest with ourselves before we can even begin to be truthful with others.

Where does the problem lie in being honest with ourselves? In the process of "selfing"—of trying to create in our own minds a permanent, autonomous, separate self—we are likely to distort what's really there. As we do so, to feel better about ourselves, often at the expense of others, we often exaggerate the positive or minimize the negative qualities we perceive in ourselves. Sometimes, we do so just a little—we tell our-selves "a little white lie." Sometimes we outright lie in very large ways to ourselves, often through the device of rationalization ("I'm not an alcoholic—you'd drink too if you had my problems"). Meditation teacher Gil Fronsdal summed this situation up neatly: "Love of truth is more important than love of self."

To pursue the ideals of a spiritual path, we must have harmony between who we are and what we say and do. If you are to follow a spiritual path, you must *never* lie to yourself under any circumstances. If you find your-self unsure of your own intentions and meanings, it is very important that you find a spiritual mentor with whom you can explore what is true.

For many years, Alcoholics Anonymous has been praising the necessity for truthfulness; it stresses identifying "the exact nature of our wrongs" in its Twelve Steps. Alcoholism is a disease that directly or indirectly kills and wounds millions of people every year. AA has a remarkable record of success in lifting the curse of this disease from active alcoholics. Many who have achieved and maintained sobriety avow that they can only do so through complete honesty, and it is very common at AA meetings to hear phrases such as "You are as sick as your secrets" or "You are as sick as you are secret." Many alcoholics have led lives that have wreaked havoc, often illegally, on themselves, their families, their career, their involve-ment in all aspects of society, so there is also the injunction to make *direct* amends for these wrongs "except when to do so would injure ourselves or others."

In a very real sense all beings are addicts. It's just the "substance" that varies from being to being. We do, say, or ingest something that makes us feel good—at least for the moment—so we repeat it so that we'll continue to feel good or find that good feeling again. Perhaps the source of our pleasure is not alcohol or narcotics; instead it might be ice cream, or sex, or gossiping. As we saw in the discussion of the Four Noble Truths, all of life is characterized by suffering, whose cause is grasping or clinging to something that we believe will end the dis-ease. But ironically, only when we end the clinging do we also end the suffering. Here we come full circle and see that only by being mindful and honest with ourselves about what we cling to can we let go of dis-ease and pursue the life we really want for ourselves.

What Is Truth?

Pundits may claim that "the truth will set us free," but they rarely define *truth*. Truth is not simply fact. Poet Maya Angelou said, "There's a world of difference between truth and facts. Facts can obscure truth." In truth there is no deceit, but many have used "facts"—especially statistics—to obscure the truth. The Buddha's teachings are called the Dharma, often translated as *truth*, but the meaning of *truth* here is not some metaphysical concept but rather a statement of pragmatic value about how to live life without deceit and dis-ease.

To define truth, we must look at it in its context. First, is the "true" statement not deceitful? Second, is the intention, the motivation, behind this statement skillful, nonharming? Third, is it expressed in a way that it can be understood? Fourth, is it helpful? If a statement fails to meet any of these criteria, it is not truth. It may be a fact, but it can also be a weapon.

Let's look at each of these criteria one by one.

First, truth is not deceitful. It is not fraudulent or dishonest. It is a fact that is not misleading.

The motivation behind truthfulness is nonharming. Saying "You've got the biggest wart on your nose I've ever seen!" may be true, but clearly the intention in saying it is unkind—at the very least, the statement is thoughtless. It hurts another person.

Speaking the truth in a way that can be heard and understood is also important. If the truth is spoken in an abusive or frivolous way, the hearer may simply miss that there is substance to the remarks or may experience so much aversion as to ignore them.

And finally, the truth is helpful. Telling someone they have the ugliest nose you've ever seen is in no way helpful. In contrast, a beneficial statement might be, "Has a dermatologist ever looked at the lesion on your nose?"

Harmful Truthfulness

Certain kinds of truthfulness are especially unskillful. Abusive speech—yelling and using profanity and insults—is counterproductive. Rather than using speech to communicate, it is generating an aversive reaction that has the opposite effect.

There have been all too many news items recently concerning bullying, some of which have ended with suicides. One particularly ugly video shows four adolescents bullying a grandmother who was a monitor on a school bus. They told her she was ugly, was fat, was alone in the world because everyone had killed themselves rather than be around her (one of her children had committed suicide); age is no protection against verbal assault. I was reminded of a time decades before when it was adults hurling insults at innocent, very young children who were trying to integrate a school. Some of the words a bully uses might be fact, but they are not truthfulness.

Frivolous speech may just be a means of establishing communication with someone—for example, running into a friend and saying, "Where have you been hiding yourself? I haven't seen you for ages." When the friend responds, "And how are you?" the words are also a way of making a social connection, rather than a request for a recital of ills. This kind of "speech" is problematic only when it dominates all social interaction and just fills dead air without conveying anything of meaning. It may even be a way of avoiding true communication.

Gossip is probably the most harmful form of frivolous speech—whether the rumor is true or not, it can be so destructive. A very old Jewish story makes the point well. A man in a small village goes to his rabbi, ashamed that he has been spreading (true) rumors about a neighbor. When he asks what he can do to make up for this, the rabbi tells him: "Walk to the next village. Buy a chicken. On the way back to me, pluck all its feathers." The gossiper follows these instructions exactly. When he gives the chicken to the rabbi and asks what he should do next, the rabbi tells him to retrace his steps and pick up every feather he has dropped. The man exclaims, "But that's impossible!" "Just like taking back the words you have spread around," replies the rabbi.

Talking about someone who is not present, even if what you say is true and even complimentary, may not be beneficial. Doing so indicates that you are not really in the present moment. Your listener may even think something like "Why is he singing her praises? I'm here and she's not."

Truth and Faith

There's a relationship between truthfulness and faith that is important to understand when we make the resolution to be truthful.

Faith is sometimes difficult to define. In fact, in many languages the word is a verb, rather than a noun, which makes it a bit easier to pin down. "Faithing" is doing, not just believing. In a sense, what we're striving to learn to do in this book is faithing.

There are at least three phases in faith that one metaphor communicates well. First, you tell me I can jump over that creek. I am skeptical and don't accept that kind of information with blind faith. But if you yourself then jump over the creek, that act gives me provisional faith that perhaps I can do it too. With that "faith," I then jump over the creek and achieve verified faith. I moved from doubt, to uneasy belief, to complete faith. One thing about the Buddha's teachings that appealed to me greatly was his instruction to never take his word for anything; rather, we should go out and test his teaching for ourselves. This invitation to verified faith has for me also been the wisdom of verified truth. The teachings are so practical and avoid the metaphysical realms so well that I am able to test them all until I can verify their truth.

One way I've found very useful in testing a given truth (or wisdom statement) has been to try to disprove it. When "it" is something relatively simple such as the fact that vision occurs when a sense organ has contact with an object, I can usually think the proposition through until I feel comfortable with its truth. On the other hand, when I face something as complex as "not-self," I often do research in books and other sources, then write down the arguments as I see them. For some very complex teachings, I may work with the concept—sometimes with a teacher—until it really becomes a solid, verified truth for me, which can take time I may measure in months or years.

Modern Truthfulness

We need to look at how we communicate in very broad terms, including how we talk, write, illustrate, gesture, listen, and even dress. In all these forms, we must ask if we are creating or enhancing a sense of self, if we are harming others, or if we're bringing kindness and harmony into our world.

Much written communication today is via electronic devices, and the hundreds of texting messages sent each day by an average adolescent can rarely be considered anything other than frivolous. In the extreme, they many take the form of gossip and bullying and cause real harm in the world.

Cartoons and caricatures can be amusing, and often humor can be used to deliver truth in a very skillful manner. Too often, however, they are used in unskillful and abusive ways, making fun of cultural, religious, ethnic, or age issues. They can cause others much suffering—including individuals far beyond the person who may be depicted.

Even the way we dress may be unskillful or deceitful. Think of the sexually provocative pictures very young people—trying to look older—may post on Internet social networks, which may lead them unknowingly into dangerous situations.

Sometimes a whole group dresses in a particular way as a general statement. I remember many years ago moving to southern California, where I found myself surrounded by other young people in sandals and tie-dye shirts and beads. I thought, "Oh, here are my people, the political outsiders like me." Wrong. They were, through their clothes, making a fashion statement, not a political one.

Practice and Reflection: Truthfulness

1. In your next long conversation with a friend, before you speak, be sure that each statement is true, useful, and can be heard.

2. What does the word *truthful* mean to you?

3. What motivates you to be truthful?

4. Is there harmony between what you say and what you do?

5. Is it ever acceptable to lie? To others? To yourself?

6. Do you have personal secrets to enable you to continue with actions or words that may be unskillful?

7. Do you ever gossip in the workplace? In social situations? At home?

8. Do you ever use profanity or abusive language? What is its effect on others?

9. Sit quietly for ten minutes and do a meditation practice using the repetition of these phrases as the object of your concentration/mindfulness. As you silently repeat the phrases, do so slowly enough to feel what each one would be like in your life:

   May I be happy.
   May I be healthy.
   May I live in safety.
   May I be truthful to myself and others.

13.
Resolve

Resolution: May I resolve to practice for my deepest liberation.

Mantra: May I resolve to practice for the benefit of all beings.

RESOLVE, OR DETERMINATION, is inseparable from the other perfections. It is the underlying reason one undertakes, and is cultivated simultaneously with, each of these spiritual ideals. But though we practice it alongside the other perfections, it's worth taking a little time to focus on resolve specifically. By the time we have worked with truthfulness, we are ready to focus on the perfection of resolve.

Dhammapala states directly that the perfection of resolve is the unshakable determination to undertake activity for the good of others, accompanied by compassion and skillful means. He also stresses that resolve has the characteristic of determination upon the requisites of enlightenment; its function is to overcome their opposites; its manifestation is unshakableness in that task. To put it simply: one must have steadfast resolve to undertake the perfection of the paramis, with the overall goals being compassion and liberation for all beings.

Whenever a historical description of the perfections is undertaken, in order to give a sense of how long it takes to accomplish their purification, the tale of the monk Sumedha is commonly told. Many, many eons before the time of the historical Buddha, there lived a young monk named Sumedha, the son of a very wealthy family. After his parents' deaths, Sumedha inherited their wealth and began to reflect deeply on the meaning of having so many material things. All of his family—his parents, his aunts and uncles and cousins—had had such wealth, but when they died, they had left it behind. A deeply spiritual young man, he decided to give up everything material ("like a wad of phlegm," it is said) to the poorest people of his region and went up into the mountains to become a hermit-monk.

One day when Sumedha went into the nearest village with his begging bowl, he saw a great commotion. When he asked what was happening, he was told that the buddha of that age, Dipankara, was coming to the town. Sumedha was deeply moved by the prospect of seeing a real buddha and hurried to join the crowd. As Dipankara approached a muddy place on the path, Sumedha threw himself on the ground and covered the mud with his long black hair so that the buddha would not have to step in the mud. The two men then made a contact that many feel changed the world. Sumedha was so motivated by this encounter that he resolved that one day he too would be a buddha, and Dipankara recognized this resolve and swore that after many lifetimes of purifying the perfections, Sumedha would be born as Siddhartha Gautama, the historical Buddha. Over countless subsequent lifetimes, recounted in other Jataka Tales, the bodhisattva lived under all imaginable conditions as a human, an animal, even a tree to be able to purify these spiritual ideals.

This story is not meant to discourage you; when we undertake to cultivate the perfections, we are not trying to set ourselves up for eons of challenges dependent upon reincarnation. Rather, please view it as encouragement. If we have steadfastly tried to cultivate the perfections as we've read the earlier chapters of this book, we have reached the point of making an "unshakable" resolve. We have firmly dedicated ourselves to a life that is a reflection of our spiritual practice and is dedicated to liberation and compassion for all beings. You can be proud.

Let's review briefly the resolutions we've made so far:

1. Generosity: We've resolved to open our hearts to give and to receive with joy and ease.
2. Ethical Integrity: We've resolved to be mindfully virtuous in thoughts, words, and actions, to be a gift to ourselves and the beings around us.
3. Renunciation: We've resolved to renounce and let go of anything that obstructs liberation and compassion for all beings.
4. Wisdom: We've resolved that with discernment and insight we will shape choices that lead to compassion and liberation.
5. Wise Effort: We've resolved to awaken and sustain the perfections to energize our lives.
6. Patience: We've resolved to be patient and forgiving when self-centered fear or anger arises, accepting things just as they are.
7. Truthfulness: We've resolved to be truthful with ourselves so that there is harmony between what we say, what we do, and who we are.

Are we ready now for resolve #8, to practice for our own deepest liberation and for the benefit of all beings? What does this determination mean for us?

Resolve to Work toward Liberation

In its broadest concept, what we seek liberation *from* is the belief in a separate, autonomous, permanent "self." In chapter 2, we explored the teaching that there is no such self but rather collectives, or aggregates, that together make up what we consider ourselves. I always found the term *aggregates* off-putting. It sounded like I was a composite of a variety of compressed stones. But even that metaphor works.

Nevertheless, a small voice says, when I look in the mirror every morning, *I* am there, and when I see you walking down the street I can recognize you because *you* are there. True—relatively, conventionally speaking. *I* am recognizably there, and so are *you*. But what I see is not permanent or unchanging—if it were, children would never grow up and people would never age and die or even change their minds about anything. Ultimately, the conventional "self" I think I see is not an independent element *separate* from the other so-called aggregates of which I am composed. In one tale, the Buddha used the example of a chariot. He said that we can point to an axle of the chariot, but that isn't the chariot. We can point to the wheels, but they aren't the chariot. We can point to the reins, but they aren't the chariot. Only when all the necessary chariot aggregates are assembled do we have an object that we call a chariot.

When you consider the list of aggregates—material form, feeling, perception, mental formations (thoughts and emotions), and consciousness—a striking factor is that none is permanent. Each one is constantly changing. In the Four Noble Truths, the Buddha identified attachment, or clinging, to that which is impermanent as the source of suffering, and he iterated that our task is to let go of whatever we cling to. He also noted that there are four attachments that cause the most suffering: to sense pleasures, to ideas and opinions, to rites and rituals, and—above all—to self. Interestingly, the Buddha would not say whether a soul exists or not, nor would he confirm the existence of a god or any other metaphysical concept. The point was that *attachment* to a self caused suffering.

The Buddha taught the not-self doctrine not as a metaphysical assertion but as a strategy for gaining release from suffering: If one uses the concept of not-self to dis-identify oneself from all phenomena, one goes beyond the reach of all suffering and stress. When we truly realize that we are a verb, not a noun, we are on the path to liberation. And when we can see that all other beings—and things—similarly do not have a self, we can experience the interconnectedness with all beings and bring compassion into our spiritual path. As we've noted often, the Buddha stressed that he taught one thing only: suffering and the end of suffering. Think about it. He is said to have lived lifetime after lifetime for the sole purpose of ending suffering, which means that he had a single motivation—a single resolution—through all these challenges: compassion to end the suffering for all beings everywhere.

Resolve to Practice Compassion

One of the most interesting depictions of compassion is the female deity Kuan Yin, who is sometimes referred to as "the observer of the cries of the world." She is sometimes shown with a thousand arms to embrace the suffering of the world, and on the palm of each hand is an eye, which sees the suffering. We may not have a thousand eyes, but with the two we have, we can look around our world and see suffering everywhere around us—if we have the courage to look, to see it, and to not be overwhelmed by it.

When we resolve to begin our practice of compassion, we must begin with ourselves and those closest to us. Meditation teacher Marcia Rose tells a tender story of holding her infant son and experiencing a trembling of the heart—she felt the connection and intimacy of the moment but also had a sense of the suffering that her son would encounter in his lifetime.

When we feel that empathetic trembling of the heart that is compassion, we can have the unconditional courage to accept its existence by turning again to our understanding of not-self, of emptiness. We—none of us—has been singled out for suffering. It is the nature of the human condition that there be dis-ease, and when we can recognize its universality, we dissolve the separation from other beings and experience true compassion.

Vietnamese master Thich Nhat Hanh has pointed out that in many languages the word *compassion* is a verb. But there must be the caution that compassion be accompanied by wisdom—as we discussed in chapter 9, Manjushri, the embodiment of wisdom, is often paired with Avalokiteshvara, the embodiment of compassion, the other "wing of awakening." Unbridled compassion without wisdom is codependency, which helps no one. Wisdom understands the cause of suffering and what is necessary to end it. When we are strongly motivated by wisdom and compassion, we have the quality of heart that allows us to resolve to alleviate the pain of all. But again, it is best to start with ourselves. When we have the wisdom, we are able to let in the dis-ease, because we know its cause, we know that it is impermanent, and we know that it is impersonal.

✣ Take a few minutes now to do a brief compassion meditation.

1. First, contemplate compassion, described by the Buddha as a trembling of the heart in the face of another's pain. It is very important to distinguish compassion from its "near enemy"—pity. In compassion, we open our hearts to empathetic caring for another; pity always presupposes a separation, a duality, an inequality in power that negates our interconnectedness through *dukkha* ("I'm okay, but you're not").

2. Focus on the phrase "May I let go of suffering and its causes," and direct this wish to yourself. Meditatively repeat this phrase for about ten minutes, slowly enough to really understand its meanings.

3. Choose a similiar phrase, such as "May you be free of pain" or "May you be free of suffering," to direct toward someone else. You may repeat the phrase as many times as you wish each time you encounter someone who is suffering (such as a homeless person or someone in physical or emotional pain), or you may visualize someone specific, perhaps in a hospital or prison, and direct the phrases to her or him.

All around us are situations worthy of our compassion, but we must be mindfully present to come close enough to let the pain in; mindfulness is the tool that enables us to experience compassion. The Dalai Lama, whom many believe is the reincarnation of Avalokiteshvara, has said, "If you want others to be happy, practice compassion. If you want to be happy, practice compassion." And he frequently quotes verses by Shantideva in *A Guide to the Bodhisattva's Way of Life*:

> For as long as space endures
> And for as long as living beings remain,
> Until then may I too abide
> To dispel the misery of the world.

The verse above and our wishes from the compassion practice are resolutions. Mindfulness of the resolutions we make when we are on the meditation cushion and when we are living out normal life meld and provide an ongoing structure for our spiritual practice.

Resolve to Practice

By now you'll realize that if you choose to make your life your spiritual practice, you need the motivation and discipline to establish a practice that supports this goal. Here are the factors to consider:

- Establishing a daily practice is critical. You don't have to set a length of time for each session, but it is helpful if your plan is to sit at the same time and the same place each day, if only for a few minutes.
- Pick a quiet place and time when you are unlikely to be interrupted. You may want to set up an altar with an image that is meaningful for you. (Some use an image of the Dalai Lama or the Buddha as a reminder of what is possible, but certainly you could use a Christian image, or an honored benefactor or relative.) Other items often chosen for an altar include representatives of the four elements: water (in a cup or vase), earth (a flower), air (incense), and fire (a candle). You yourself are in the fifth element: space.
- Sit in a way that you are comfortable, in a posture you can hold for as long as you plan to sit. Mats and cushions as well as benches are available easily on the Internet. Or you can fold over a pillow and sit in the middle of your bed. Or you can sit in a chair. Any of these choices is right if it works for you.
- Establish your intention for that sitting. It may be a simple statement such as "I intend to practice for the benefit of all beings." You may wish to use a more formal practice such as taking the refuges.

The traditional phrasing of taking the refuges:

> I take refuge in the Buddha.
> I take refuge in the Dharma.
> I take refuge in the Sangha.

Some alternative phrases for taking the refuges might be as follows:

> May I take refuge in my capacity to awaken.
> May I take refuge in the ways of living that bring about my freedom and happiness.
> May I feel open to all those who can support me on this path of freedom.

- Establish a time for how long you plan to meditate. Begin mindfulness practice either following your breath (see chapter 4) or using the metta phrases (see chapter 14).
- When you have finished sitting, acknowledge your effort and dedicate the merit of your practice to the benefit of all beings.

Practice and Reflection: Resolve

1. Have you truly connected with a deep desire for spiritual practice?

2. What holds you back from making this connection and this commitment?

3. Do you believe that you have a separate and autonomous self?

4. Do you feel that you can be liberated from the "burden of self"?

5. Can you open yourself to experience your own pain and to be compassionate with yourself?

6. Can you open yourself with empathy to the pain of others?

7. Do you ever feel overwhelmed by the pain in the world? How do you handle this feeling?

8. Are you willing to undertake a daily mindfulness practice?

9. Sit quietly for ten minutes and do a meditation practice using the repetition of these phrases as the object of your concentration/mindfulness. As you silently repeat the phrases, do so slowly enough to feel what each one would be like in your life:

> May I be happy.
> May I be healthy.
> May I live in safety.
> May I resolve to practice for the benefit of all beings.

14.

Loving-Kindness

Resolution: May cultivating metta practice concentrate my mind and open my heart.

Mantra: May loving-kindness define my relationships with others.

SO YOU'VE REACHED THE POINT where you say, "Okay, I want my life to be my spiritual practice. How do I do that?" No matter how diligently we've practiced the first eight perfections, it still may feel like something's been left out of the instruction manual. And it has: the last two perfections, which are our daily "default practices" that enable us to carry out the others. These are loving-kindness (or *metta*) and equanimity (which we'll discuss in chapter 15). Making these two practices part of daily life is the key to our spiritual comfort.

The Heart of Metta Practice

If you've developed a daily mindfulness practice following your breath, you may wonder why I'm suggesting that you add loving-kindness practice to it. The answer is quite simple: These two meditation practices facilitate and enhance each other. The powerful concentration and mindfulness we cultivate as we are following our breath, as we practice vipassana, strengthen our loving-kindness practice; there's no real metta without mindfulness. The openness, purification, and spaciousness of heart-mind we create by doing metta increase our capacity for insight while we are practicing vipassana—as well as while we are doing loving-kindness practice itself.

Vipassana teacher Sylvia Boorstein tells a story that well illustrates how these two kinds of practice can work together. One day Sylvia was invited to come to her grandson's first-grade class to talk about meditation. Trying to use terms that would be meaningful to six-year-olds, instead of referring to "concentration" or "mindfulness," she talked about "paying attention." One bright young boy asked a lot of questions and finally asked, "But if you're *not* paying attention, how do you *know* you're not paying attention?" Sylvia thought for a moment, then answered, "When I'm not paying attention, I'm not as kind."

Similarly, the Dalai Lama has said, "My religion is kindness." A heart inclined to kindness is very much an aid in including metta as part of our spiritual path; metta expresses our deepest intentions for happiness for all beings and melds with the compassion that is one of our ultimate goals in cultivating the perfections.

Dhammapala explains the sequence of metta among the perfections, following resolve, this way:

> (a) because loving-kindness perfects the determination to undertake activity for the welfare of others; (b) in order to list the work of actually providing for the welfare of others right after stating the determination to do so, for "one determined upon the requisites of enlightenment abides in loving-kindness"; and (c) because the undertaking (of activity for the welfare of others) proceeds imperturbably only when determination is unshakable.

Some other characteristics of metta practice are evident in one story of how it originated. According to this tale, when the Buddha sent a group of monks into the forest to meditate, they were set upon by tree demons. The monks were terrified and came running back, trembling, to ask the Buddha to send them somewhere else. He told them that instead he would teach them a practice that would protect them against fear of any threat. He taught them metta practice, and when they returned to the forest, the demons were so disarmed by the change in the monks that the tree spirits became their servants. Here we can see metta overcoming fear, instilling confidence and a sense of refuge, and being a source of radical transformation for the monks. It can bring the same benefits to us.

In addition, one of the most remarkable transformations we can experience is the feeling of freedom and spaciousness that pervades our consciousness when we either make metta our primary practice or use it in conjunction with our vipassana practice. Sharon Salzberg, whose wonderful book *Lovingkindness* is the standard "field manual" for those of us who practice metta, uses an image from one of the Buddha's discourses to show how we can increase our spaciousness to accommodate daily difficulties this way:

> Imagine taking a very small glass of water and putting into it a teaspoon of salt. Because of the small size of the container, the teaspoon of salt is going to have a big impact on the water. However, if you approach a much larger body of water, such as a lake, and put into it that same teaspoonful of salt, it will not have the same intensity of impact, because of the vastness and openness of the vessel receiving it. Even when the salt remains the same, the spaciousness of the vessel receiving it changes everything.

Loving-kindness practice can make our "vessel" so spacious that we can absorb the daily difficulties that inevitably come to us with little obvious change of equanimity. It can be an extremely positive tool when we are in challenging situations. For example, when I ride the subway in New York City or get stuck on a highway in a traffic jam, I send metta to all those around me. When I developed a chronic illness and spent a lot of time in hospitals, I was a regular metta machine, sending it to myself and other patients and their families. Metta is also my companion on retreats. If someone in the lunch line is moving glacially, I send them metta. When I'm having difficulty walking to the meditation hall, I send metta to myself. Doing so immediately puts me at ease. For me, metta practice in even small doses is my medicine for the ills that come up during daily life.

Formal Metta Practice

Metta practice is a concentration practice, but instead of focusing on our breath or footsteps, we use as the object of our concentration a certain set of phrases that describe what we would wish for ourselves and all beings. But metta practice is much more than the rote recitation of phrases. Even as we concentrate our minds, we also open our hearts in a practice that is purifying and transformational. You may not have any of the positive feelings of the phrases at first. Don't worry: you are planting seeds for loving-kindness to arise.

We formally practice metta by mentally sending our phrases to several categories of individuals and groups. How long you will be doing metta determines how long you spend repeating these phrases for each category. If, for example, you are doing a one-day metta retreat, you might spend an hour with each category. In a week-long metta retreat, you might spend a day on each. In longer retreats, you might spend a week or a month on each. If you are not on retreat, you may decide to use the first or last ten minutes of your sitting practice to send metta to yourself and others.

In preparation, find a comfortable sitting position that you can hold for a half hour or so. If you slouch, you will find it hard to stay focused or perhaps even awake, so put some energy into sitting erectly. Should pain arise in this position, distracting you from repeating the phrases, adjust your posture to one that is more comfortable. See if you can remember to smile as you begin each metta session.

Forgiveness Practice

Before actually beginning metta practice, it's a good idea to spend a few minutes contemplating forgiveness, because it is hard to generate metta if you have negative feelings toward others or yourself. I invite you to repeat each of the following phrases to yourself three times.

> If anyone has harmed me intentionally or unintentionally
> by word or deed, may I forgive them.
> If I have harmed anyone intentionally or unintentionally
> by word or deed, may they forgive me.
> If I have harmed myself intentionally or unintentionally
> by word or deed, may I forgive myself.

Metta Phrases

Once you have completed forgiveness practice, you can begin formal metta practice. I suggest using these four phrases:

> May I be safe and protected from inner and outer harm.
> May I be peaceful and happy.
> May I take care of myself wisely.
> May I accept myself completely just as I am in this
> present moment.

Sending Metta to Ourselves

We begin by sending metta first to ourselves—the Buddha said that no one is more deserving of our loving-kindness than we are ourselves. Say each phrase to yourself slowly enough that you can imagine how it feels when it is true. For example, the first phrase is *May I be safe and protected from inner and outer harm.* See if you can imagine what it feels like to be totally free of fear of harm. Then recite the next phrase. When you've gone through all four phrases, begin again.

When metta practice was taught by the Buddha nearly 2,600 years ago, the premise was that we would start with the easiest person to send metta to and progress to increasingly challenging categories: ourselves, a benefactor, a beloved friend, a neutral person, a difficult person, and finally all beings everywhere. With each category that seems challenging to us, we begin by thinking about something positive about the person— some kind or generous act or words. And we can find something positive about just about anyone.

But the sequence of beginning with ourselves may prove difficult. We may have complex or negative feelings about ourselves. So begin by thinking about some positive things about yourself. If you still have problems, visualize yourself when you were very young and send metta to that child. If this still seems difficult, repeat the phrases while remembering a specific picture of yourself as a child. Below we'll look again at some of the challenges we may encounter sending metta to ourselves or a difficult person.

Benefactor

Once you've directed metta toward yourself for a while, begin directing your phrases to someone who has affected your life positively and toward whom you feel gratitude. You should choose someone toward whom you have only positive feelings—perhaps a teacher—rather than a life partner or parent, toward whom your feelings may be more complicated. We generally select someone who is still alive because the connection is stronger, but I know people who use a grandparent or spiritual figure who is no longer alive. They generally believe that that person still exists in some realm and that they can make the connection to them.

Beloved Friend

Begin this practice by sending metta to yourself for a few minutes. If this is difficult, consider sending the metta to yourself and your benefactor together for a few minutes. Then direct your phrases toward someone for whom you have warm feelings (your concentration will be clearer if this is not a person with whom you have a sexual relationship). People sometimes select a grandchild or a pet for this category. Just observe whether you are experiencing positive emotions as you work with this category. If you aren't, don't worry—just keep saying the phrases.

Neutral Person

Begin with yourself for a few minutes, then direct your phrases to a neutral person. Meditators often are surprised to find how few people do not elicit some kind of positive or negative feelings. Among the people I have chosen as "my" neutral person were the supermarket checkout person for a line I never stand in and, on a retreat, a person sitting several rows in front of me whose face I cannot see. The surprise about sending metta to a neutral person over time is that we realize our feelings for them have changed and now are positive. Many times on retreat, I've sat there sending metta to the back of someone's head almost by rote—until the day that person doesn't show up for a sit. Then I find myself worrying if the person is all right or is sick or has left the retreat or if I should tell someone. Much to my surprise, caring about this faceless person has sneaked into my heart-mind, and I realize that she or he represents all the people around the world whom I do not know but send metta to.

Difficult Person

Begin with yourself for a few minutes, then direct your phrases to a difficult person. In some practices, this person is known as "the enemy." When you first begin doing metta, choose someone who is not *too* difficult to practice on. Picking the most difficult person you've ever known will illustrate clearly how the hindrance aversion can totally derail your ability to concentrate. If you do feel great aversion for this person, before you begin directing the phrases to him or her, spend a few minutes calling to mind good qualities the person has or good acts the person has done. Another strategy for being able to work with a particularly difficult person is to imagine that you are standing next to him or her and to send metta to both of you ("May we be safe...").

This practice can be especially helpful in challenging workplace or family situations. Some years ago, a man worked for me who was one of the most difficult people I have ever managed and at the same time one of the most creative, for many of the same reasons. I found myself in a position where I could fire him, but I could not tell him what to do. I did not want to fire him, but I did want to lessen my feelings of resentment so that I could be collegial enough to support him in what he did well. I spent a few minutes doing metta for him as soon as I came into the office each day, and the practice enabled us to work together well, and profitably, for years.

All Beings

Begin with yourself for a few minutes, then direct your phrases to all beings everywhere, saying something like "May we be happy..." Some people get more specific in repeating the phrases here. You might say, "All beings everywhere..." or "All beings in the six directions..."

You also might send the phrases, for example, to people in Africa or Iraq or Afghanistan, or you might direct metta to beings with no legs, two legs, four legs, then multiple legs.

Feelings of Resistance

On my first intensive metta retreat, I was quite amazed to realize on the last day that the feelings that arose for me were no different whether I was sending metta to my beloved friend, my neutral person, or my enemy. I felt at a cellular level the absence of separation. In this light, let me address something that may have come up for you—resistance to full-heartedly sending wishes for happiness to yourself or another. There are several stories of times when the Dalai Lama has been meeting with Western teachers or students and the subject of low self-worth has come up. In the earliest one, a group of teachers spent several hours trying to explain low self-esteem to him. In another, a man at a retreat he visited asked how to deal with self-hatred. The Dalai Lama in no uncertain terms told his listeners that low-self worth is wrong—that each of us naturally has a radiant and loving mind.

It's like the old (possibly apocryphal) story of someone asking Michelangelo how he created the statue of David. Michelangelo replied, "I just took a large piece of granite and chipped away everything that wasn't David." Sometimes we have to chip away at our encrustations too. We have to ask ourselves if we are willing to renounce our bad feelings about ourselves. To quote Sharon Salzberg:

> For a true spiritual transformation to flourish, we must see beyond this tendency to mental self-flagellation. Spirituality based on self-hatred can never sustain itself. Generosity coming from self-hatred becomes martyrdom. Morality born of self-hatred becomes rigid repression. Love for others without the foundation of love for ourselves becomes a loss of boundaries, codependency, and a painful and fruitless search for intimacy. But when we contact, through meditation, our true nature, we can allow others to also find theirs.

Using Metta with Other Practices

As we begin to contact our true nature through meditation, we can find it quite helpful to integrate vipassana and metta. For example, I begin all sittings by taking the refuges and end them with metta—perhaps sending wishes to only a few people, or a sick friend, or all beings.

Some people make metta their whole practice, some go on retreats that practice only metta, some use metta as a way to stabilize their body and mind at the beginning of a sitting, and others use it at the end of each sitting as a way of dedicating their practice to all beings. Once, on a metta retreat, I combined a devotional practice of taking the three refuges with metta at the beginning of each sitting:

Taking refuge in the Buddha: loving myself.

Taking refuge in the Dharma: seeing myself clearly.

Taking refuge in the Sangha: honoring myself in all other beings.

In recent years, as my admiration for the ten perfections has deepened, I have integrated phrases related to them into my metta practice. For instance, the "Practice and Reflection" entries at the end of each chapter of part II is an example of how I have done this. I have done long retreats devoted entirely to this integration, and the appendix at the end of this book is a suggested guide for doing a self-retreat on metta and the perfections.

Practice and Reflection: Loving-Kindness

1. For one week, spend as much of each day as you can sending metta to a specific person. For the reasons given above, it is helpful to start with oneself briefly after Day 1, and to do a brief period of sending to oneself before going to the other people on our list at each sitting.

Day	Category
1	Oneself
2	Benefactor
3	Beloved Friend
4	Neutral Person
5	Difficult Person
6	All Beings
7	Oneself

Did you have difficulty sending metta to yourself? Did the last two phrases ("May I take care of myself wisely" and "May I accept myself completely just as I am in this present moment" or something similar) help?

1. Why did you choose the benefactor your did? The beloved friend?

2. Did you have difficulty finding a neutral person? Is this because you have strong feelings toward everyone around, or do you have neutral feelings toward many people?

3. Did your level of concentration change when you came to the difficult person?

4. Did you generalize in sending metta to all beings, or did you focus on particular regions or cultures?

5. When you send metta to yourself again on the last day, have your feelings about yourself changed?

6. Sit quietly for ten minutes and do a meditation practice using the repetition of these phrases as the object of your concentration/mindfulness. As you silently repeat the phrases, do so slowly enough to feel what each one would be like in your life:

> May I be happy.
> May I be healthy.
> May I live in safety.
> May loving-kindness define my relationships
>   with others.

15.
Equanimity

IN MANY TEACHINGS, the Buddha referred to four qualities that are so
positive that they are known as the "heavenly abodes," or *brahmaviharas*
in Pali—loving-kindness, compassion, sympathetic joy, and equanimity—
the balance among our body, heart, and mind.

Thinking about the brahmaviharas always reminds me of my first
experience with Buddhism as an adult. Many years ago a friend invited
me to a presentation on "How to Bring Peace to the World." I was an
aging social activist and this seemed like the opportunity for me to con-
nect with some others in New York City with similar interests. When we
arrived at the hall, it was crowded with people wearing sandals and beads,
and I felt quite at home. After a little while, a slight Vietnamese monk
took the stage. For the next three hours, Thich Nhat Hanh taught us
mindfulness meditation, with the caution that we couldn't bring peace
to the world until we first brought peace to ourselves. With equanimity,
we could face any challenge. Without it, we could face down none.

Equanimity—calmness and balance of the heart-mind in the face of
stress—is an important quality in all the Buddha's teachings. For example,

equanimity is the final quality listed in both the brahmaviharas and the ten perfections. In both instances equanimity is the ultimate characteristic that arises from cultivating the others and in fact functions to strengthen all of the heart-mind characteristics that lead to liberation. During recent windstorms, I thought of equanimity as I watched Chinese elms through my window: I saw the tops of the trees whipped around frenziedly by the wind and branches being snapped off, but when I looked at the base of the trunk near the ground, it was unmoved even during the most fierce buffeting. Equanimity metaphorically relocates us from the branches to the trunk.

It's important to distinguish equanimity from other states such as indifference and apathy, which cause contraction and withdrawal from what is happening, and which are founded upon ignorance. Equanimity, on the other hand, is founded upon wisdom and enables us to see reality as it is—no matter how pleasant or unpleasant—and to be present with composure and nonreactivity. This does not mean that we do not respond—just that we can do so much more wisely, and we do not re-act out old karma.

Equanimity, like other skillful characteristics of the heart-mind, can be cultivated, and I'd like to share with you some of my most important experiences with equanimity practice. Life happens, and mine has been quite challenging in recent years, due primarily to my health and my partner's health. I've worked with brahmavihara practices, especially loving-kindness and compassion, and such perfections as patience during all this time, and they've brought me much peace.

Late one spring, a few days before I left for a retreat, my partner's problems—which had previously been attributed to an old back injury and unsuccessful spine surgery two and a half years before—were diagnosed as multiple sclerosis. Her actual state had not changed; the only thing that was different in our lives was that now we had a label, and she insisted that I go ahead and attend the retreat, which I really needed for recharging my spiritual batteries.

I arrived at the retreat at a beautiful mountain refuge, sat down on my cushion, and began to follow my breath. In no time at all, my hindrance of choice—restlessness—swept in and I began to compulsively and repeatedly plan things I could do to help my partner: put up more handrails, get a raised planter for herbs, and on and on and on. No matter how much effort I put into concentration on my breath, monkey mind ran rampant. Two breaths and my mind was off and running again. Sometimes when I have trouble concentrating on my breath, I switch to metta practice—reciting the loving-kindness phrases often helps. But this time, it suddenly occurred to me that the words I most needed to work with were not loving-kindness but rather equanimity. Here are the phrases I began to work with:

> I am the maker of my karma,
> The inheritor of my karma,
> The owner of my karma.
> My happiness or unhappiness depends upon
> My own intentions and actions,
> Not upon my or your wishes.

> You are the maker of your karma,
> The inheritor of your karma,
> The owner of your karma.
> Your happiness or unhappiness depends upon
> Your own intentions and actions,
> Not upon your or my wishes.

Before I look at the individual phrases, it's important to recall the groundwork on two critical and complementary wisdom teachings of the Buddha: karma and the impersonality of life, discussed in chapter 3.

It's important to remember that because karma is intentional action, many occurrences in life are not karmic. The chronic illnesses of unknown origin that both my partner and I suffer from are not "bad karma." A child born with severe birth defects is not suffering the effects of karma. However, my two closest friends, both heavy smokers even after the danger of smoking became well known, died of lung cancer.

Because they both knew the consequences of their action and continued to smoke, their premature deaths were karmic. Although I have not smoked for twenty-plus years, I consider the heart disease I developed karmic because I was fully aware of the risk I was taking by smoking for as long as I did.

We also need to remember that although many illnesses are not karmic, the ways we respond to them are. For example, I developed chronic vasculitis a dozen years ago, was in and out of hospitals, took some very toxic drugs, and for much of the time was quite physically disabled. If I had just sat around weeping and complaining that "life isn't fair," I would just have been planting the seeds for more suffering. Yes, there were times that I wept and complained. But I also spent several summers lying under a lilac bush cultivating a moss garden by plucking out grass because that was something I could do lying down when I couldn't sit up. As my health improved, I could stand and walk for short distances, but not up into the mountains I loved so much. So I bought a horse and a ladder, climbed on Bonita, and let her carry me up the trails. (I still do.) I was still sick—I am still sick—but in terms of karma and dukkha I didn't make things worse.

The Buddha describes the way we can exacerbate our suffering in this way: In our lives, pain comes to us like we're shot by an arrow. But then we start to tell ourselves stories about our pain, and it's like we are shooting ourselves with a second arrow into the same wound. This teaching follows the adage that pain is inevitable but suffering is optional. Sometimes the best way to handle suffering is with humor. After my accident with the horse last summer, both my partner and I were wheelchair-bound. One morning we sat side by side laughing at our predicament: neither of us could reach the shelf with the oatmeal on it, and we had to settle for yogurt for breakfast.

Which leads to the second teaching point: life/pain is not personal. Everyone gets sick, gets old, dies. These states are not karma in and of themselves; they happen to everyone. The Buddha made this point in several other metaphors: When it rains, the drops fall on everyone and everything; rain isn't selective. When the sun shines, it shines on every-one; it too is not personal in singling out who it will shine upon. The specific events and situations of our lives are much less important than how we relate to them. When we can relate with equanimity, we are much happier.

Equanimity Practice: Whose Karma?

Equanimity practice, like metta, is a concentration practice that uses set phrases rather than the breath as the object. Like metta, these phrases can be directed to categories of beings or can focus on oneself or another. And like metta, the practice concentrates the mind as it eases and opens the heart. Let's look more closely at the phrases I suggest using.

I am the maker of my karma.

Probably everything that ever happened in the world had to happen for me to be right here, right now. Our worlds are cobbled together from others' national, family, and individual karma—and from our own. When we see the world as it really is, we see the karma of all times playing out.

The only karma we have any control over is our own for the future. Seeing this fact is at the heart of equanimity. It is also the motivation for cultivating mindfulness to the best of our ability. Only the present moment is real. The only time we have a choice in our lives is this very moment. When we are mindful in the moment of what we are doing and the consequences of our actions, we can craft a life that is as skillful as we can make it, not bringing harm or unhappiness to ourselves or others. With every intentional action, we are generating karma. Whether it is "bad" or "good"—skillful or unskillful—depends upon our mindfulness, wisdom, and intentions.

Let me give one example. In New York, a woman who was an active alcoholic worked for me. She came back to the office from lunch each day quite drunk. Her work was mediocre and causing hardship to others.

Her life situation was such that she was surrounded by "enablers" and never really felt the consequences of her drinking. Only her liver knew. So I talked with her in the only way I could as an employer: I told her that her drinking was causing problems in the office, that this was a medical problem, not a moral issue, and that I would support her seeking treatment, inpatient or outpatient, whatever would work best for her. I told her that if her behavior did not change, she would be terminated. She continued to come in drunk after lunch, and I fired her on the basis of her poor work performance. This was the first time she had to really look at her life. A week later she stopped drinking, and after she was sober for six months she applied for her old job—and got it. My firing her may have looked unskillful; she said I was cruel, and I certainly caused her suffering. But to not have fired her would have really been unskillful, causing great stress to other employees and enabling her to self-destruct. I evaluated the situation and then took the best, most skillful action I could for all parties involved—which is all you can do to make for yourself the best karma you can. Because you're making your own: it's an inside job.

I am the inheritor of my karma.

Whenever I commit an intentional action, I am the heir to its consequences, sooner or later. If I cut someone off in traffic, I may experience their road rage almost immediately. Sometimes it takes longer for the effects. I was part of a small sangha in New York City, and when a deeply divisive problem arose, I thought I was taking the high road by insisting that certain practices change. The result, over time, was that the sangha evaporated. I learned from that experience, so that when I moved to Taos, I made the commitment to try to serve Taos Mountain Sangha in any way I could—financially as a sustaining member, by offering talks from time to time, by showing up for events like board planning meetings, etc. Over the past few years, I hope I have helped others' practice; I certainly have strengthened my own, and made some wonderful Dharma friends in the meantime—ongoing good karma.

I am the owner of my karma.

My karma is my karma. I may have inherited karmic situations from my family and culture, but what I do with that inheritance is my responsibility. It is very common for people who were abused as children to in turn abuse their own children. When they own up to their intentional actions, they can change their future karma—and that of their children.

When I first got involved with Buddhism, my understanding of karma was very shallow: I only seemed to be able to understand karmic results of actions that I took after I had learned what karma is. During one of the most painful periods of my life, I felt that I had been very badly used—and I blamed another person for my suffering in a breakup. One of the most beautiful things we learn through Buddhist practice is our interconnection with all beings, and that nothing separates us from other beings as much as blame. In our isolation, we enhance our own suffering. It took me years to realize that if I had understood karma before the relationship began, I would never have gotten into it. My actions were unskillful and caused great suffering to others. When I knew now what I didn't know then, I was able to own my karma, and to make changes in my own life.

> My happiness or unhappiness depends upon
> My own intentions and actions,
> Not upon my or your wishes.

When we find ourselves in deep spiritual pain, we have somehow shot ourselves with that second arrow. The fact of karma is that we cannot change the past, but if we are present in this moment, we can change how we react to the past and therefore change our future karma. The good news is that it's never too late.

One of the Buddha's most dramatic teachings about how one can change is the story of Angulimala: Angulimala was a brutal killer who slayed all living beings in his path and wore a garland of fingers of his human victims around his neck. One day, as the Buddha walked to a village to collect alms, many people tried to stop him, warning that Angulimala was somewhere ahead on the road. But the Buddha kept going. Suddenly Angulimala jumped out of the woods and began to follow the Buddha. No matter how hard Angulimala ran, he couldn't catch up. When Anguli-mala realized what had happened, he had a flash of enlightenment and became one of the Buddha's most devoted followers—so changed that those who had feared him in the past didn't recognize him. As he learned that it was his intentions not his wishes that set his karmic course for the future he underwent such a dramatic transformation that the monks renamed him "Doer of No Harm."

Equanimity and Others

A very important aspect of my equanimity practice in recent years has been not just directing it toward myself but also toward my ill partner. The stress of our evolving situation has brought up both the best and the worst in me.

The worst goes back to my childhood. When I was about five, my father went off to fight in WWII, and my mother convinced me that I was responsible for her happiness. I became a lifelong fixer, trying desperately to ensure the happiness of people I cared for. Being a fixer in this sense in my new situation with my partner would be terribly unskillful and would cause dis-ease for both of us. For myself, I had to not go under the delusion that I could change another person's reality enough to make them happy. In the same way that I did not come between my alcoholic employee and reality, I had to not come between my partner and her reality. She had to face her situation—her MS—and make her own karma in the way she responded to it. So I began to direct these phrases to her.

> You are the maker of your karma,
> The inheritor of your karma,
> The owner of your karma.
> Your happiness or unhappiness depends upon
> Your own intentions and actions,
> Not upon my wishes for you.

As my concentration deepened and the phrases felt more and more integrated in my consciousness, I began to experience a deep sense of relief and confidence that I could be a skillful person in this situation. I could do for her what she could not do for herself, but I could also refrain from shielding her from the great teacher of her illness.

Things went along well for a few days, but I began to get uneasy—it seemed like in directing the equanimity phrases toward her, I was saying something like "It's your problem." So I began to send her metta after each round of three or four equanimity phrases—and to send myself metta after I directed equanimity phrases to myself. This union was absolutely miraculous in the strength and calmness it gave me. There was absolutely no separation between myself and my partner spiritually when I practiced this way.

Several days after I returned home from the retreat where I was so challenged by her diagnosis, my partner and I together attended what was supposed to be a week-long metta retreat offered by Marcia Rose. Perhaps because I had told Marcia of my experience, Marcia devoted the first four days to traditional loving-kindness and the last three to equanimity. The result was like a wonderful alchemy for my partner and me; we both ended up on the same page of the Dharma in our practice. Dhammapala explains the sequential relationship of metta, the other perfections, and equanimity this way:

"Equanimity is mentioned immediately after loving-kindness: because equanimity purifies loving-kindness... Even though the mind has been softened with the moisture of loving-kindness, without equanimity one cannot purify the requisites of enlightenment and cannot dedicate one's requisites of merit along with their results to furthering the welfare of beings... Thus equanimity is indispensable to the practice of all the other paramis.

There is little I can add to these words, written by a Sri Lankan in the fifth century. If you want your life to be your spiritual practice, set yourself the goals of compassion and liberation for all beings through purification of the ten perfections, united and supported by equanimity. The goal of spiritual practice is to see clearly and accept the world around us without greed, hatred, and aversion. This clarity and acceptance could also be phrased as wisdom and compassion—seeing the world just as it is without grasping or pushing away. When we can achieve this goal, we face the world with happiness, with equanimity.

All the brahmaviharas and the Buddha's teachings on impermanence, karma, and interconnectedness come together in equanimity. We can cultivate equanimity by repeating a phrase such as "May we accept all things just as they are." This does not mean that we never take action, for example, to change the ills of society but rather that we see clearly what they are and accept that they exist, whether we want to try to change them or not. Each time we practice the perfections, we do this. Each time we go into a voting booth, we do this.

Practice and Reflection: Equanimity

1. In your opinion, what is the relationship between generosity and equanimity?

2. Between ethical integrity and equanimity?

3. Between letting go and equanimity?

4. Between wisdom and equanimity?

5. Between wise effort and equanimity?

6. Between energy and equanimity?

7. Between patience and equanimity?

8. Between truthfulness and equanimity?

9. Between loving-kindness and equanimity?

10. Sit quietly for ten minutes and do a meditation practice using the repetition of these phrases as the object of your concentration/mindfulness. As you silently repeat the phrases, do so slowly enough to feel what each one would be like in your life:

    May I be happy.
    May I be healthy.
    May I live in safety.
    May I be nonreactive to the unexpected
        changes of life.

Appendix:
A Self-Retreat on Metta and the Perfections

IN A VERY REAL SENSE, all retreats—no matter where or how formally structured—are self-retreats. Only our heart-mind is on the one cushion, and only we know what is there.

Sustained daily practice is the most powerful way to develop our spiritual life. When we can make the time, doing a retreat—alone or with a group, in our own home or at a refuge—can greatly enhance our practice and our personal growth. I often take a weekend or four or five days alone to do self-retreats, but I've also worked with retreat teachers to formulate my own "self-retreat" within the context of a formal retreat. For me, this has the great value of practicing with the support of the group, hearing Dharma talks, and having interviews with teachers to work through whatever is coming up for me.

Recently, with the teachers' permission and input, I did a four-week perfections/metta self-retreat while with the Mountain Hermitage annual retreat in Taos, New Mexico. Before the retreat, I had drafted most of this book, had created the resolutions and mantras I would use, and had tentatively outlined a schedule for how I would practice each day. At some times I practiced with the retreat sangha (at a 5:30 AM sit and Metta Sutta chant; at Dharma talks). The rest of the time, I set my own schedule and format and practiced alone. This guide is the result of what worked best for me. How you use it will depend upon the time you have available—a day a week; a weekend; some consecutive days in or out of a formal retreat. If you do join a retreat, it's important to talk with the teacher ahead of time and seek her or his guidance and permission. I've outlined below ten sessions, but how you work out the times depends upon what is available to you. The times, the sequence, and the phrases used are suggestions only, and you should modify them to suit your needs. If you do choose to alter or substitute the phrases, do so before you start; do not change them during the course of your retreat.

As you are making these teachings your own, there are also invitations for you to free-write: For ten minutes (or twenty or thirty if you choose) write about one of the questions in the practice section of that chapter. Don't lift your pen or pencil, don't edit, don't correct—just write for the entire time you've set aside. At the end of this short exercise, ask yourself what was important that you wrote about, what you omitted, and how this topic can be integrated into your practice. Sean Murphy and Natalie Goldberg for many years have taught workshops that combine meditation and writing. Goldberg's book *Writing Down the Bones: Freeing the Writer Within* is a supportive guide for this type of writing. To the guidelines above, she adds: "Lose control. Don't think. Don't get logical. Go for the jugular. (If something comes up in your writing that is scary or naked, dive right into it. It probably has lots of energy.)... First thoughts are also unencumbered by ego, by the mechanism in us that tries to be in control, tries to prove the world is permanent and solid, enduring and logical."

Session 1: Generosity

I suggest beginning your retreat with the customary taking of the refuges, using either the traditional words or an alternate or else chanting them in Pali. Repeat whatever version you use three times. You may also find it helpful to take the refuges at the beginning of each session of this retreat.

The traditional phrases:

I take refuge in the Buddha.
I take refuge in the Dharma.
I take refuge in the Sangha.

Alternative phrases for taking the refuges:

May I take refuge in my capacity to awaken.
May I take refuge in the ways of living that bring about my
    freedom and happiness.
May I feel open to all those who can support me on this path
    of freedom.

The refuges in Pali (you can chant these entirely on one note):

Buddham saranam gacchami	I go for refuge to the Buddha
Dhammam saranam gacchami	I go for refuge to the Dhamma
Sangham saranam gacchami	I go for refuge to the Sangha
Dutiyam pi	A second time
Buddham saranam gacchami	I go for refuge to the Buddha
Dhammam saranam gacchami	I go for refuge to the Dhamma
Sangham saranam gacchami	I go for refuge to the Sangha
Tatiyam pi	A third time
Buddham saranam gacchami	I go for refuge to the Buddha
Dhammam saranam gacchami	I go for refuge to the Dhamma
Sangham saranam gacchami	I go for refuge to the Sangha

1. *First sitting: vipassana for 20 minutes.*
   Take your usual meditation posture, state your intention for this sitting, and follow your breath as you usually do in your mindfulness meditation.

2. *Reading.*
   Read chapter 6, "Generosity."

3. *Free-write for 10–30 minutes each on the following questions.*
   - How do you feel when you have acted generously? Do you ever feel needy?
   - How do you practice nonharming in order to give the gift of safety to those in your family? Your community? Your nation? Your planet?

4. *Meditate using these metta/perfections phrases as your object of concentration for as many 40-minute periods as you can.*
   May I be happy.
   May I be healthy.
   May I live in safety.
   May I give with joy.

5. *Break up periods of sitting meditation with 20 minutes of walking meditation during which you repeat only the last of the above phrases with each step.*
   May I give with joy.

6. *Reflect on the full list of resolutions, rereading each of the phrases at least three times. Try to relate generosity to each of the perfections as you consider it.*

   1. **Generosity:** May my heart be open to give and to receive with joy and ease.

2. **Ethical Integrity:** May ethical integrity in thoughts, words, and actions be my gift to myself and the beings around me.

3. **Renunciation:** May I renounce and let go of anything that does not lead to liberation and compassion for all beings.

4. **Wisdom:** With discernment and insight, may I make choices that lead to compassion and liberation.

5. **Wise Effort:** May I awaken and sustain the perfections in my life.

6. **Patience:** May I be patient and forgiving when self-centered fear or anger arises, accepting things just as they are.

7. **Truthfulness:** May I be truthful with myself so that there is harmony between what I say, what I do, and who I am.

8. **Resolve:** May I resolve to practice for my deepest liberation.

9. **Loving-Kindness:** May cultivating metta practice concentrate my mind and open my heart.

10. **Equanimity:** Balanced in body, heart, and mind, may I be nonreactive to what arises and passes away.

7. *Final sitting: vipassana for 20 minutes.*
   Appreciate your efforts, sit quietly while focusing on your breath, then get a good night's sleep.

Session 2: Ethical Integrity

1. *First sitting: vipassana for 20 minutes.*
   Take your usual meditation posture, state your intention for this sitting, and follow your breath as you usually do in your mindfulness meditation.

2. *Reading.*
   Read chapter 7, "Ethical Integrity."

3. *Free-write for 10–30 minutes each on the following questions.*
   - How strictly do you observe the precept to abstain from harming living beings?
   - Can intentional actions be viewed as skillful or unskillful, or do you believe that some actions are inherently good or evil? Why?

4. *Meditate using these metta/perfections phrases as your object of concentration for as many 40-minute periods as you can.*
   May I be happy.
   May I be healthy.
   May I live in safety.
   May I give freedom from fear to all beings.

5. *Break up periods of sitting meditation with 20 minutes of walking meditation during which you repeat only the last of the above phrases with each step.*
   May I give freedom from fear to all beings.

6. *Reflect on the full list of resolutions, rereading each of the phrases at least three times. Try to relate ethical integrity to each of the perfections as you consider it.*

   1. **Generosity:** May my heart be open to give and to receive with joy and ease.

2. **Ethical Integrity:** May ethical integrity in thoughts, words, and actions be my gift to myself and the beings around me.

3. **Renunciation:** May I renounce and let go of anything that does not lead to liberation and compassion for all beings.

4. **Wisdom:** With discernment and insight, may I make choices that lead to compassion and liberation.

5. **Wise Effort:** May I awaken and sustain the perfections in my life.

6. **Patience:** May I be patient and forgiving when self-centered fear or anger arises, accepting things just as they are.

7. **Truthfulness:** May I be truthful with myself so that there is harmony between what I say, what I do, and who I am.

8. **Resolve:** May I resolve to practice for my deepest liberation.

9. **Loving-Kindness:** May cultivating metta practice concentrate my mind and open my heart.

10. **Equanimity:** Balanced in body, heart, and mind, may I be nonreactive to what arises and passes away.

7. *Final sitting: vipassana for 20 minutes.*
Appreciate your efforts, sit quietly, then get a good night's sleep.

Session 3: Renunciation

1. *First sitting: vipassana for 20 minutes.*
   Take your usual meditation posture, state your intention for this sitting, and follow your breath as you usually do in your mindfulness meditation.

2. *Reading.*
   Read chapter 8, "Renunciation."

3. *Free-write for 10–30 minutes each on the following questions.*
   - Describe how you perceive that each sense is a sense—not a self.
   - Is it easy or difficult for you to exchange a lesser, immediate happiness for a greater, long-term happiness—to exchange candy for gold? What is the most challenging example of wanting immediate gratification for you?

4. *Meditate using these metta/perfections phrases as your object of concentration for as many 40-minute periods as you can.*
   May I be happy.
   May I be healthy.
   May I live in safety.
   May I let go of ever harming other beings.

5. *Break up periods of sitting meditation with 20 minutes of walking meditation during which you repeat only the last of the above phrases with each step.*
   May I let go of ever harming other beings.

6. *Reflect on the full list of resolutions, rereading each of the phrases at least three times. Try to relate renunciation, or letting go, to each of the perfections as you consider it.*

   1. **Generosity:** May my heart be open to give and to receive with joy and ease.

2. **Ethical Integrity:** May ethical integrity in thoughts, words, and actions be my gift to myself and the beings around me.

3. **Renunciation:** May I renounce and let go of anything that does not lead to liberation and compassion for all beings.

4. **Wisdom:** With discernment and insight, may I make choices that lead to compassion and liberation.

5. **Wise Effort:** May I awaken and sustain the perfections in my life.

6. **Patience:** May I be patient and forgiving when self-centered fear or anger arises, accepting things just as they are.

7. **Truthfulness:** May I be truthful with myself so that there is harmony between what I say, what I do, and who I am.

8. **Resolve:** May I resolve to practice for my deepest liberation.

9. **Loving-Kindness:** May cultivating metta practice concentrate my mind and open my heart.

10. **Equanimity:** Balanced in body, heart, and mind, may I be nonreactive to what arises and passes away.

7. *Final sitting: vipassana for 20 minutes.*
Appreciate your efforts, sit quietly, then get a good night's sleep.

Session 4: Wisdom

1. *First sitting: vipassana for 20 minutes.*
Take your usual meditation posture, state your intention for this sitting, and follow your breath as you usually do in your mindfulness meditation.

2. *Reading.*
Read chapter 9, "Wisdom."

3. *Free-write for 10–30 minutes each on the following questions.*
   - Do you believe that it is possible to pursue enduring happiness for both oneself and others at the same time? Why or why not? How or how not?
   - Do your sources of livelihood—including investments and retirement funds—harm anyone? If you discovered they do, would you change these sources to ones that are nonharming? Why or why not?

4. *Meditate using these metta/perfections phrases as your object of concentration for as many 40-minute periods as you can.*
   May I be happy.
   May I be healthy.
   May I live in safety.
   May my choices be wise and compassionate.

5. *Break up periods of sitting meditation with 20 minutes of walking meditation during which you repeat only the last of the above phrases with each step.*
   May my choices be wise and compassionate.

6. *Reflect on the full list of resolutions, rereading each of the phrases at least three times. Try to relate wisdom to each of the perfections as you consider it.*

1. **Generosity:** May my heart be open to give and to receive with joy and ease.

2. **Ethical Integrity:** May ethical integrity in thoughts, words, and actions be my gift to myself and the beings around me.

3. **Renunciation:** May I renounce and let go of anything that does not lead to liberation and compassion for all beings.

4. **Wisdom:** With discernment and insight, may I make choices that lead to compassion and liberation.

5. **Wise Effort:** May I awaken and sustain the perfections in my life.

6. **Patience:** May I be patient and forgiving when self-centered fear or anger arises, accepting things just as they are.

7. **Truthfulness:** May I be truthful with myself so that there is harmony between what I say, what I do, and who I am.

8. **Resolve:** May I resolve to practice for my deepest liberation.

9. **Loving-Kindness:** May cultivating metta practice concentrate my mind and open my heart.

10. **Equanimity:** Balanced in body, heart, and mind, may I be nonreactive to what arises and passes away.

7. *Final sitting: vipassana for 20 minutes.*
   Appreciate your efforts, sit quietly, then get a good night's sleep.

Session 5: Wise Effort

1. *First sitting: vipassana for 20 minutes.*
Take your usual meditation posture, state your intention for this sitting, and follow your breath as you usually do in your mindfulness meditation.

2. *Reading.*
Read chapter 10, "Wise Effort."

3. *Free-write for 10–30 minutes each on the following questions.*
   - What are the most personally challenging unskillful qualities, intentions, words, and actions you must *guard against*?
   - What are the most personally challenging unskillful qualities, intentions, words, and actions you must *abandon*?
   - What are the most personally important skillful qualities, intentions, words, and actions you must *develop*?
   - What are the most personally important skillful qualities, intentions, words, and actions you must *maintain*?

4. *Meditate using these metta/perfections phrases as your object of concentration for as many 40-minute periods as you can.*
   May I be happy.
   May I be healthy.
   May I live in safety.
   May goodness energize my life.

5. *Break up periods of sitting meditation with 20 minutes of walking meditation during which you repeat only the last of the above phrases with each step.*
   May goodness energize my life.

6. *Reflect on the full list of resolutions, rereading each of the phrases at least three times. Try to relate wise effort to each of the perfections as you consider it.*

1. **Generosity:** May my heart be open to give and to receive with joy and ease.

2. **Ethical Integrity:** May ethical integrity in thoughts, words, and actions be my gift to myself and the beings around me.

3. **Renunciation:** May I renounce and let go of anything that does not lead to liberation and compassion for all beings.

4. **Wisdom:** With discernment and insight, may I make choices that lead to compassion and liberation.

5. **Wise Effort:** May I awaken and sustain the perfections in my life.

6. **Patience:** May I be patient and forgiving when self-centered fear or anger arises, accepting things just as they are.

7. **Truthfulness:** May I be truthful with myself so that there is harmony between what I say, what I do, and who I am.

8. **Resolve:** May I resolve to practice for my deepest liberation.

9. **Loving-Kindness:** May cultivating metta practice concentrate my mind and open my heart.

10. **Equanimity:** Balanced in body, heart, and mind, may I be nonreactive to what arises and passes away.

7. *Final sitting: vipassana for 20 minutes.*
Appreciate your efforts, sit quietly, then get a good night's sleep.

Session 6: Patience

1. *First sitting: vipassana for 20 minutes.*
   Take your usual meditation posture, state your intention for this sitting, and follow your breath as you usually do in your mindfulness meditation.

2. *Reading.*
   Read chapter 11, "Patience."

3. *Free-write for 10–30 minutes each on the following questions.*
   - Can you cultivate skillful qualities if you do not have patience?
   - What kinds of situations test your patience the most? Is anger a component of your reaction?

4. *Meditate using these metta/perfections phrases as your object of concentration for as many 40-minute periods as you can.*
   May I be happy.
   May I be healthy.
   May I live in safety.
   May I be patient and forgiving to all.

5. *Break up periods of sitting meditation with 20 minutes of walking meditation during which you repeat only the last of the above phrases with each step.*
   May I be patient and forgiving to all.

6. *Reflect on the full list of resolutions, rereading each of the phrases at least three times. Try to relate patience to each of the perfections as you consider it.*

   1. **Generosity:** May my heart be open to give and to receive with joy and ease.

   2. **Ethical Integrity:** May ethical integrity in thoughts, words, and actions be my gift to myself and the beings around me.

3. **Renunciation:** May I renounce and let go of anything that does not lead to liberation and compassion for all beings.

4. **Wisdom:** With discernment and insight, may I make choices that lead to compassion and liberation.

5. **Wise Effort:** May I awaken and sustain the perfections in my life.

6. **Patience:** May I be patient and forgiving when self-centered fear or anger arises, accepting things just as they are.

7. **Truthfulness:** May I be truthful with myself so that there is harmony between what I say, what I do, and who I am.

8. **Resolve:** May I resolve to practice for my deepest liberation.

9. **Loving-Kindness:** May cultivating metta practice concentrate my mind and open my heart.

10. **Equanimity:** Balanced in body, heart, and mind, may I be nonreactive to what arises and passes away.

7. *Final sitting: vipassana for 20 minutes.*
Appreciate your efforts, sit quietly, then get a good night's sleep.

Session 7: Truthfulness

1. *First sitting: vipassana for 20 minutes.*
   Take your usual meditation posture, state your intention for this sitting, and follow your breath as you usually do in your mindfulness meditation.

2. *Reading.*
   Read chapter 12, "Truthfulness."

3. *Free-write for 10–30 minutes each on the following questions.*
   - What motivates you to be truthful?
   - Is it ever acceptable to lie? To others? To yourself?

4. *Meditate using these metta/perfections phrases as your object of concentration for as many 40-minute periods as you can.*
   May I be happy.
   May I be healthy.
   May I live in safety.
   May I be truthful with myself and others.

5. *Break up periods of sitting meditation with 20 minutes of walking meditation during which you repeat only the last of the above phrases with each step.*
   May I be truthful with myself and others.

6. *Reflect on the full list of resolutions, rereading each of the phrases at least three times. Try to relate truthfulness to each of the perfections as you consider it.*

   1. **Generosity:** May my heart be open to give and to receive with joy and ease.

   2. **Ethical Integrity:** May ethical integrity in thoughts, words, and actions be my gift to myself and the beings around me.

3. **Renunciation:** May I renounce and let go of anything that does not lead to liberation and compassion for all beings.

4. **Wisdom:** With discernment and insight, may I make choices that lead to compassion and liberation.

5. **Wise Effort:** May I awaken and sustain the perfections in my life.

6. **Patience:** May I be patient and forgiving when self-centered fear or anger arises, accepting things just as they are.

7. **Truthfulness:** May I be truthful with myself so that there is harmony between what I say, what I do, and who I am.

8. **Resolve:** May I resolve to practice for my deepest liberation.

9. **Loving-Kindness:** May cultivating metta practice concentrate my mind and open my heart.

10. **Equanimity:** Balanced in body, heart, and mind, may I be nonreactive to what arises and passes away.

7. *Final sitting: vipassana for 20 minutes.*
   Appreciate your efforts, sit quietly, then get a good night's sleep.

Session 8: Resolve

1. *First sitting: vipassana for 20 minutes.*
   Take your usual meditation posture, state your intention for this sitting, and follow your breath as you usually do in your mindfulness meditation.

2. *Reading.*
   Read chapter 13, "Resolve."

3. *Free-write for 10–30 minutes each on the following questions.*
   - Have you truly connected with a deep desire for spiritual practice?
   - Do you feel that you can be liberated from the "burden of self"?

4. *Meditate using these metta/perfections phrases as your object of concentration for as many 40-minute periods as you can.*
   May I be happy.
   May I be healthy.
   May I live in safety.
   May I resolve to practice for the benefit of all beings.

5. *Break up periods of sitting meditation with 20 minutes of walking meditation during which you repeat only the last of the above phrases with each step.*
   May I resolve to practice for the benefit of all beings.

6. *Reflect on the full list of resolutions, rereading each of the phrases at least three times. Try to relate resolve to each of the perfections as you consider it.*

   1. **Generosity:** May my heart be open to give and to receive with joy and ease.

   2. **Ethical Integrity:** May ethical integrity in thoughts, words, and actions be my gift to myself and the beings around me.

3. **Renunciation:** May I renounce and let go of anything that does not lead to liberation and compassion for all beings.

4. **Wisdom:** With discernment and insight, may I make choices that lead to compassion and liberation.

5. **Wise Effort:** May I awaken and sustain the perfections in my life.

6. **Patience:** May I be patient and forgiving when self-centered fear or anger arises, accepting things just as they are.

7. **Truthfulness:** May I be truthful with myself so that there is harmony between what I say, what I do, and who I am.

8. **Resolve:** May I resolve to practice for my deepest liberation.

9. **Loving-Kindness:** May cultivating metta practice concentrate my mind and open my heart.

10. **Equanimity:** Balanced in body, heart, and mind, may I be nonreactive to what arises and passes away.

7. *Final sitting: vipassana for 20 minutes.*
   Appreciate your efforts, sit quietly, then get a good night's sleep.

Session 9: Loving-Kindness

1. *First sitting: vipassana for 20 minutes.*
   Take your usual meditation posture, state your intention for this sitting, and follow your breath as you usually do in your mindfulness meditation.

2. *Reading*
   Read chapter 14, "Loving-Kindness."

3. *Free-write for 10–30 minutes each on the following questions.*
   - Describe how you felt sending metta to yourself?
   - Was your concentration interfered with when you sent metta to a difficult person? Did any of the hindrances arise for you?

4. *Meditate using these metta/perfections phrases as your object of concentration for as many 40-minute periods as you can.*
   May I be happy.
   May I be healthy.
   May I live in safety.
   May loving-kindness define my relationships with others.

5. *Break up periods of sitting meditation with 20 minutes of walking meditation during which you repeat only the last of the above phrases with each step.*
   May loving-kindness define my relationships with others.

6. *Reflect on the full list of resolutions, rereading each of the phrases at least three times. Try to relate loving-kindness to each of the perfections as you consider it.*

   1. **Generosity:** May my heart be open to give and to receive with joy and ease.

2. **Ethical Integrity:** May ethical integrity in thoughts, words, and actions be my gift to myself and the beings around me.

3. **Renunciation:** May I renounce and let go of anything that does not lead to liberation and compassion for all beings.

4. **Wisdom:** With discernment and insight, may I make choices that lead to compassion and liberation.

5. **Wise Effort:** May I awaken and sustain the perfections in my life.

6. **Patience:** May I be patient and forgiving when self-centered fear or anger arises, accepting things just as they are.

7. **Truthfulness:** May I be truthful with myself so that there is harmony between what I say, what I do, and who I am.

8. **Resolve:** May I resolve to practice for my deepest liberation.

9. **Loving-Kindness:** May cultivating metta practice concentrate my mind and open my heart.

10. **Equanimity:** Balanced in body, heart, and mind, may I be nonreactive to what arises and passes away.

7. *Final sitting: vipassana for 20 minutes.*
Appreciate your efforts, sit quietly, then get a good night's sleep.

Session 10: Equanimity

1. *First sitting: vipassana for 20 minutes.*
   Take your usual meditation posture, state your intention for this sitting, and follow your breath as you usually do in your mindfulness meditation.

2. *Reading.*
   Read chapter 15, "Equanimity."

3. *Free-write for 10–30 minutes each on the following questions.*
   - What is the relationship between generosity and equanimity?
   - What is the relationship between ethical integrity and equanimity?

4. *Meditate using these metta/perfections phrases as your object of concentration for as many 40-minute periods as you can.*
   May I be happy.
   May I be healthy.
   May I live in safety.
   May I be nonreactive to the unexpected changes of life.

5. *Break up periods of sitting meditation with 20 minutes of walking meditation during which you repeat only the last of the above phrases with each step.*
   May I be nonreactive to the unexpected changes of life.

6. *Reflect on the full list of resolutions, rereading each of the phrases at least three times. Try to relate equanimity to each of the perfections as you consider it.*

   1. **Generosity:** May my heart be open to give and to receive with joy and ease.

2. **Ethical Integrity:** May ethical integrity in thoughts, words, and actions be my gift to myself and the beings around me.

3. **Renunciation:** May I renounce and let go of anything that does not lead to liberation and compassion for all beings.

4. **Wisdom:** With discernment and insight, may I make choices that lead to compassion and liberation.

5. **Wise Effort:** May I awaken and sustain the perfections in my life.

6. **Patience:** May I be patient and forgiving when self-centered fear or anger arises, accepting things just as they are.

7. **Truthfulness:** May I be truthful with myself so that there is harmony between what I say, what I do, and who I am.

8. **Resolve:** May I resolve to practice for my deepest liberation.

9. **Loving-Kindness:** May cultivating metta practice concentrate my mind and open my heart.

10. **Equanimity:** Balanced in body, heart, and mind, may I be nonreactive to what arises and passes away.

7. *Final sitting: vipassana for 20 minutes.*
Appreciate your efforts, sit quietly, then get a good night's sleep.

Suggested Reading

BOOKS RELATED TO THE PERFECTIONS, ONLY THE FIRST OF WHICH IS RECOMMENDED FOR NEWCOMERS TO BUDDHISM:

Boorstein, Sylvia. *Pay Attention for Goodness' Sake: The Buddhist Path of Kindness* (2007).

Acariya Dhammapala. *A Treatise on the Paramis*, translated from the Pali by Bhikkhu Bodhi (2005).

Aitken, Robert. *The Practice of Perfection: The Paramitas from a Zen Buddhist Perspective* (2012).

Altman, Donald. *Living Kindness: The Buddha's Ten Guiding Principles for a Blessed Life* (2009).

Gyatso, Kelsang. *The Bodhisattva Vow: The Essential Practices of Mahayana Buddhism* (1995).

Shantideva. *A Guide to the Bodhisattva's Way of Life*, translated by Stephen Batchelor (1999).

BOOKS OF BUDDHIST TEACHINGS APPROPRIATE FOR DAILY LIFE:

Byrom, Thomas, trans. *The Dhammapada*. Sacred Teachings edition (2001).

Cowell, E. B. *The Jataka* (1895).

Goldstein, Joseph. *Insight Meditation: The Practice of Freedom* (2012).

———. *Mindfulness: A Practical Guide to Awakening* (2013).

Gunaratana, Bhante Henepola. *Mindfulness in Plain English,* revised edition (2011).

Hanh, Thich Nhat. *The Diamond That Cuts Through Illusion* (2010).

———. *The Heart of Understanding* (1987).

———. *Old Path White Clouds: Walking in the Footsteps of the Buddha* (1991).

———. *Present Moment, Wonderful Moment: Mindfulness Verses for Daily Living* (2011).

Kabat-Zinn, Jon. *Wherever You Go, There You Are: Mindfulness Meditation in Everyday Life* (2009).

Salzberg, Sharon. *Lovingkindness: The Revolutionary Art of Happiness* (2011).

Rahula, Walpola. *What the Buddha Taught* (2007).

Smith, Jean. *Now! The Art of Being Truly Present* (2004).

———. *The Beginner's Guide to Walking the Buddha's Eightfold Path* (2002).

Thanissaro Bhikkhu. *Dhammapada: A Translation* (1998).

Weisman, Arinna, and Jean Smith. *The Beginner's Guide to Insight Meditation* (2011).

Whitmyer, Claude, ed. *Mindfulness and Meaningful Work: Explorations in Right Livelihood* (1994).

BOOKS OF THE PALI CANON:

Bodhi, Bhikkhu. *The Connected Discourses of the Buddha: A Translation of the Samyutta Nikaya* (2009).

———. *In the Buddha's Words: An Anthology of Discourses from the Pali Canon* (2005).

———. *The Middle Length Discourses of the Buddha: A Translation of the Majjhima Nikaya* (2013).

———. *The Numerical Discourses of the Buddha: A Translation of the Anguttara Nikaya* (2012).

Walshe, Maurice. *The Long Discourses of the Buddha: A Translation of the Digha Nikaya* (2005).

Index

Page numbers followed by "(2)" indicate two discussions.

About the Author

JEAN SMITH is the author or editor of numerous successful books on Buddhism. A longtime associate of the Insight Meditation Society, she serves on the board of directors of the Mountain Hermitage in Taos, New Mexico, and is a frequent guest teacher at sanghas in New Mexico. She can be reached online at buddhabooksmith.com and soberkarma.com.

Other Books by Jean Smith

from Wisdom Publications

The Beginner's Guide to Insight Meditation
with Arinna Weisman
256 pages | $15.95 | ebook $11.62

"The perfect starter kit for people curious about Buddhism."
—*Publishers Weekly*

Now!
The Art of Being Truly Present
208 pages | 5.5 x 6.5 inches | $14.00

"Every saying in this book is a good tool for meditation."
—*Eastern Horizon*

12 Steps on Buddha's Path
Bill, Buddha, and We
208 pages | $12.95 | ebook $9.43

"This book is an excellent introduction to 12-Step and Buddhist principles, and an insightful synthesis of the two traditions. Anyone seeking
to understand recovery from a Buddhist perspective will find it to be a
trustworthy and illuminating guide."
—Kevin Griffin, author of *One Breath at a Time: Buddhism
and the Twelve Steps*

About Wisdom Publications

WISDOM PUBLICATIONS is the leading publisher of classic and contemporary Buddhist books and practical works on mindfulness. Publishing books from all major Buddhist traditions, Wisdom is a nonprofit charitable organization dedicated to cultivating Buddhist voices the world over, advancing critical scholarship, and preserving and sharing Buddhist literary culture.

To learn more about us or to explore our other books, please visit our website at www.wisdompubs.org. You can subscribe to our eNewsletter, request a print catalog, and find out how you can help support Wisdom's mission either online or by writing to:

Wisdom Publications
199 Elm Street
Somerville, Massachusetts 02144 USA

You can also contact us at 617-776-7416 or info@wisdompubs.org.

Wisdom is a 501(c)(3) organization, and donations in support of our mission are tax deductible.

Wisdom Publications is affiliated with the Foundation for the Preservation of the Mahayana Tradition (FPMT).

More Books from Wisdom Publications

Enlightenment to Go
Shantideva and the Power of Compassion to Transform Your Life
David Michie
288 pages | $17.95 | ebook $13.08

One of *Spirituality and Practice*'s Best Spiritual Books of 2011.

Free Yourself
Ten Life-Changing Powers of Your Wise Heart
Carolyn Hobbs
270 pages | $17.95 | ebook $11.99

"Carolyn Hobbs offers readers a guide for awakening heart wisdom that arises from her years of healing work with others. *Free Yourself* will help us to inhabit our lives with the fullness of loving presence."
—Tara Brach, PhD, author of *Radical Acceptance*

Awakening Through Love
Unveiling Your Deepest Goodness
John Makransky
Foreword by Lama Surya Das
280 pages | $16.95 | ebook $12.35

"A rare combination of fine Buddhist scholarship and deep meditative understanding. John Makransky has done us all a great service."
—Joseph Goldstein, author of *A Heart Full of Peace*

The Grace in Aging
Awaken as You Grow Older
Kathleen Dowling Singh
240 pages | $17.95 | ebook $11.99

"Don't grow old without it."—Rachel Naomi Remen, MD, author of
Kitchen Table Wisdom

Christian Insight Meditation
Following in the Footsteps of John of the Cross
Mary Jo Meadow, Kevin Culligan, Daniel Chowning
288 pages | $16.95

"This book lucidly shows us how much Christian insight meditation
supports the purifying path to God and self-knowledge. I highly recommend this book for anyone seeking a serious, contemplatively oriented
meditation practice aimed at a truer, freer life available to God's grace
moment by moment."
—Tilden Edwards, Founder and Senior Fellow, Shalem Institute for
Spiritual Formation

Selfless Love
Beyond the Boundaries of Self and Other
Ellen Jikai Birx
248 pages | 5x8" | $15.95 | ebook $11.99

"In my opinion, love is the common element that all of humanity
strives for. Ellen's exposition of selfless love shows how we can attain
this. A wonderful book. I heartily recommend it."
—Bernie Glassman, cofounder of the Zen Peacemaker Order and
author of *The Dude and the Zen Master*